Salad Leaves
for All Seasons

ORGANIC GROWING FROM POT TO PLOT

Charles Dowding

With drawings by Jennifer Johnson

Green Books

First published in 2008
by Green Books Ltd
Foxhole, Dartington,
Totnes, Devon TQ9 6EB

Printed in the UK on Corona Natural 100% recycled paper
by TJ International Ltd

British Library Cataloguing in Publication Data
available on request

ISBN 978 1 900322 20 1

Salad Leaves
for All Seasons

Contents

Contents (continued)

For Susie

Acknowledgements

To all the people who have helped me grow vegetables over the years, especially:

Victor Crutchley, David Sanders and Bepp, Lisa, Brian, Anne, Pippa Beckett, David Godfrey, Wallee McDonnell, Susie Corbett, Bill Craster, Sara Frears, Paul and Ulli from Germany, Hilda Denham, Nicky Hembridge, Vicky Matthews, Finny Fox-Davies, Kate Plowman, Greg Morter, Nicole Leathley, Heather Mora, Emily Evans, Geoff Branson, Rosie Stott and Alex Simon.

Introduction

Since starting vegetable growing in 1981, I have become more and more fascinated by salad. Lettuce was one of the first crops in 1983, from my newly created acre and a half of raised beds in the old farm orchard. In May and June of that year I sold many dozens of butterhead lettuce hearts, some in the village, where a surprised neighbour commented that there was enough flavour for her not to need any mayonnaise!

That set me wondering; where had the flavour gone in other lettuce? All I had done was to grow them in honest soil to organic standards. Over the next few years, lettuce became one of my bestsellers and also, luckily, one of the few slightly profitable crops to grow – partly because it matured so quickly, and partly because it always sold so well, in spite of the little grey slugs lurking inside many hearts (as they do…). But in those days, other salad leaves were not in demand and lamb's lettuce was almost the only different kind I grew, mostly to sell in March and April.

Moving to France in 1991 helped me to explore some new possibilities. Oddly enough the kitchen garden at our small farm grew purslane as one of its main summer weeds, far more than we could eat. Endives were often sold in local markets and pretty oak-leaved lettuce as well, but even there the locals' phrase *une salade* meant lettuce or endive heart only. There was no interest in loose leaves of rocket which after all came from Italy, or in oriental leaves from even farther away.

So my interest in the great potential of salad leaves lay dormant for a while. After returning to Britain, it was a request from Bill the Butcher in Bruton to create some bags of mixed leaves that opened my eyes to the possibilities for anyone with some soil, compost, a bit of spare room in the garden and a spirit of adventure. Since then I have enjoyed experimenting with different seeds, sowing dates, picking methods and growing media to discover new flavours, shapes and colours at all different times of year.

Salad bags from Lower Farm are now sold in many outlets within about four miles, enough distance to provide enough customers for everything I can grow. Picking takes much more time than growing and is a demanding job, bent over in the cool of the dawn; two of us gather leaves before and just after breakfast then mix, wash and pack them immediately so that people can eat them that day or pubs can serve them for lunch. Customer feedback is enthusiastic, often emphasising the leaves' flavour and keeping ability – which is because they are healthy and alive.

In this book I offer you the information needed to grow and harvest leaves of a similar quality and variety.

The Conjuror's Hat

Salad leaves are one of the quickest and easiest vegetables you can grow. More than that, plants that are well looked after will provide long successions of harvests, without having to repeatedly sow or plant again. How to continually crop the same plants and give them a surprisingly long life – a main theme of this book – is explained in Part One. New leaves just keep appearing – it is almost magical.

Another key theme in the book is growing in small spaces and containers, which can be impressively productive. You may also find yourself appreciating the growing beauty of your range of salad plants, as much as their abundant contributions to the table.

The leaves you pick will also be full of seasonal characteristics, reflecting how different salads give of their best at particular times of year. Appreciating this calendar of salad seasons, explained in Part Two, will help towards more success in growing healthy plants. In Part Three I offer a tour of the great range of salad possibilities, and all necessary information on how to obtain the best from them. Lastly, in Part Four there is an explanation of how to use covered spaces to extend the season of growth and to ensure a steady supply of leaves for much of the winter, as well as earlier outdoor harvests in the spring.

Charles Dowding
Lower Farm
March 2008

Part One

GROWING LEAVES

Chapter 1

High Yields, Small Spaces, Special Methods

Learning new tricks

You do not need a large garden to grow good amounts of leaves. Small beds or containers can produce surprisingly large harvests, especially if they are in full light. Whatever the size of your growing area, the important thing is to make the most of it.

THE KEYS TO SUCCESS

Many salad plants can be long-lived when they are correctly chosen for the season and well tended. This is a key aspect of successful growing, enabling you to enjoy high production from small areas. Which plants are grown and how they are picked is as important as your general sowing and growing techniques (see Chapter 2, pp.16-22 for more details) and careful choosing and tending of plants really can make even containers and window boxes capable of producing enough leaves to be a good asset to the table.

Sowing at the right moment also makes an important difference. The season, the moon and the weather all play a part and becoming more aware of their changes will bring you extra knowledge and health, not least from having more leaves to eat.

FIRST STEPS

Keep your initial purchases small and simple. Catalogues and shops are full of expensive accessories that are not strictly necessary. The main things you will need are seed and/or plants, a container or bed to grow them in, some good compost, a watering-can and, above all, sufficient time to tend your plants on a regular basis. Once a growing space is set up, the main work is picking leaves.

Start in a small way, but also experiment with lots of different salad plants to see which ones grow best for you and provide leaves which you enjoy eating. Soon you will get the hang of managing an interesting range of plants at different times of year to keep those healthy harvests coming.

LARGER SPACES

If there is room outside and you want plenty of leaves, think about a bed along the lines of those in Chapter 3, pp.23-30, which, over a trial season, produced around 1-2kg weekly of mixed leaves between late April and mid-October, then rather less until Christmas. Once the materials have been sourced, new beds can be constructed quite rapidly and in almost any location – on top of grass, gravel or paved areas. An open space is better than against a wall, because more light will give better growth.

In view of the productivity of well-tended salad plants, my advice to people with large gardens is often to scale down their salad area and manage it more tightly. Valuable compost can be concentrated on a smaller space and there is less weeding and watering to do.

Larger beds are useful for those plants needing lots of room to grow, such as the wide range of hearting plants. Study the book and plan a growing space to be in line with your intended harvests.

A single bed can be kept fully productive throughout the growing season by re-sowing or re-planting as soon as gaps appear. Check the information in Part Two, pp.68-77, to see which plants are coming into their period of most productive and healthy growth, according to the time of year.

SMALLER SPACES

Small spaces can profit from the use of large containers, which may even be quite shallow for salad, as long as they are well watered in dry weather. The large round lettuce pot in Chapter 4, p.34, which yields leaves for three months off a dozen plants, has a diameter of 62cm (25"), a depth of 22cm (9") and contains about forty litres of compost. Or look at the recycled plastic window boxes which measure one metre by 20cm and are 15cm deep (39"x 8"x 6"), hold 15 litres of compost and offer worthwhile yields of leaves for a long period (see Chapter 4, pp.31-8).

The small volumes of such containers compared with gardens and raised beds, means that good quality compost must be used, both to retain as much moisture as possible, and to provide enough nutrients for steady and significant growth. Organic composts are available to meet these criteria (see *Resources*) and I feel they are the best option for achieving well-balanced, even growth and for highly nutritious leaves. Their nutrient levels can be topped up between crops with, for example, a few handfuls of comfrey and lucerne pellets; this avoids having to refill containers with new compost.

SALAD SEASONS

Best results come from appreciating which leaves grow best at which time of year. Growing plants in their right season will give you far more success than if you sow anything you fancy at any time of year. For example, spinach and lettuce grow best in the spring, purslane and basil require summer heat, endives and mizuna thrive in the autumn, while chicories, rocket and lamb's lettuce are hardy enough to provide leaves in most British winters.

A seasonal approach achieves more abundant harvests and healthier leaves, because insects that live off certain plants are only prevalent at certain times: avoid growing them in those periods and growth will be healthier.

An extra benefit of this approach is the constantly changing nature of your harvests. Salad is not the same old thing, day in day out, for months on end. April's leaves are quite different from August's, while many leaves in a bowl of late autumn salad, for example, are quite peculiar to that season and are suited to boosting your health as winter approaches.

FLAVOUR

With the changing seasons come frequent and fascinating changes in salad flavour. I have devoted a whole chapter to this subject, to whet your appetite and to illustrate the surprisingly large range of tastes to be had in a bowl of leaves.

THE BENEFITS OF ORGANIC GROWING

The main benefit in growing your own leaves is that they are eaten fresh, firm and full of flavour. Organic methods help to achieve this: firstly for healthier plants, whose growth is easier to manage, and secondly to nourish you and your family or friends with extra-nutritious food. I outline ways of constructing or assembling beds of any size that are full of well-rotted manure, compost and soil, plus a few additions for extra trace elements.

Growing plants organically and in their right season should ensure that pests are mostly absent. Occasionally aphids will appear in the spring, before ladybirds arrive to eat them, and they can simply be washed off after picking the leaves. Slugs are more problematic in certain situations, such as enclosed yards with many walls, and I offer ideas for dealing with them. Pests and disease will always be with us, so we need to work out the best way of minimising their impact. Often this is achieved more successfully by understanding how they operate and gardening accordingly, than by gardening in a more random way and having to deal with major problems that arise.

THE MOON AND UNSEEN INFLUENCES

Earthly influences are powerful, so sowing dates are governed firstly by the season and secondly by the weather.

Yet salad leaves are nearly all water, and water is massively influenced by the moon, suggesting that salad leaves grown according to the moon's phases will grow more strongly (see Chapter 7, pp.57-9).

QUALITY LEAVES, FULL OF FLAVOUR

Quality is the main reason for growing your own leaves. They will be different from most of those for sale, much livelier, brighter, crisper, more colourful and with plenty of exciting tastes to enjoy. You can create your own palette of salad flavours – have a look at Chapter 5, pp.39-46, and choose from its wide-ranging and amazingly long menu, and then use Chapter 10 (pp.78-92) to inspire you with ideas for eating them.

Chapter 2

Vital Knowledge for Successful Harvests

Less sowing, more picking

BRIEF SUMMARY

- *Sow seeds thinly for picking individual leaves, more thickly for cutting rows or clumps*

- *Wider spacings give healthier leaves over a longer time*

- *Grow in best-quality compost, or surface-dress garden soil with good compost*

- *For picking you can choose to cut baby leaves or pick medium-sized ones, depending on salad type and your preferences*

- *Harvested leaves will keep for days if cool and moist*

- *One sowing for each season can be enough to have leaves all the year round (fewer in winter)*

Although this chapter is about how to grow salad plants, it is mainly and more importantly about how to pick their leaves, for the enjoyment of:

- Regular supplies of tasty salads
- Longer-lived plants, with less need for re-sowing

HOW TO SOW SEEDS

The two main choices are between sowing directly into beds or containers, or sowing into modules or seed trays on a window sill, conservatory or greenhouse bench (see Chapter 6, pp.47-56). Direct outdoor sowings are harder to space thinly and tend to emerge as dense rows of seedlings, which then do best if thinned out a little. Module-sown seed is easier to ration out, from one seed per module for hearting lettuce to four or five for spinach, mustards and most other salads. A third possibility is thick sowings into seed trays or boxes, usually indoors, to have crops of 'micro-leaves' cut as seedlings or picked as baby leaves for pretty garnishes (see Chapter 4, pp 31-8).

Always sow into well dampened soil or compost; because salad seed is mostly small, it is best sown very shallow, half a centimetre deep or even less in the case of lettuce. Deeper sowings usually take longer to emerge and may not come up at all. The seedbed needs to be continually damp for just a few days until seed is germinated. In dull, cool conditions this means no watering at all between sowing and the first spell of fine weather. In hot summer weather, daily watering with a gentle rose will probably be necessary. Then as seedlings turn into young plants with deeper roots, intervals between watering can be extended to three or four days, allowing the surface to dry out in between, which offers less encouragement to slugs and weed seeds.

SPACING PLANTS FOR DIFFERENT HARVESTS

Most salad plants grow quite large if given space and left unpicked, but well spaced plants that are regularly picked over can crop for long periods of up to three months, depending on the time of year. Medium-sized leaves have a different flavour from baby leaves and a firmer texture, which helps them to keep well.

Thicker sowings are suitable for cutting lots of baby leaves, but will crop for a shorter period and so you will need to re-sow more often to have a continuity of salad.

Each person needs to find the system of growing and cropping which best suits his or her taste, lifestyle and garden. I have tried many methods over the decades and have enjoyed most success with a combination of three aspects of growing, two of which are intimately related to the spacing of plants:

- **Spacing plants out more than usual,** often 20-25cm (8-10") apart in all directions, enables them to live longer, develop more leaf colour, and makes picking easier. Spacing any wider gives no added benefit for salad leaves and also results in an increased growth of weeds as well as a need for extra water. Most effective use of space is made by planting 'on the square'. Imagine a grid of squares across your planting area: plant at all points where grid lines intersect, as well as into the centre of every square, to achieve an equal distance between plants in every direction (see below).

- **Picking a few of the outer leaves of all plants on a regular basis,** rather than cutting across the top of them, ensures a steady supply of leaves for the table and a longer life for plants that, through careful handling and never being allowed to grow up into large specimens, continue producing tender small- to medium-sized leaves as though in a state of suspended adolescence.

- **Sowing or planting into well composted soil.** Compost provides steady moisture and temperature, and sufficient nutrients as plants require them, all over a long period. Salad plants are not normally considered 'heavy feeders', unlike say tomatoes, but their growth is constant and is well adapted to the nutrients, water and energy that a good compost can provide.

GATHERING LEAVES

New growth is always happening from tiny leaves at the centre of the plant, so these should be left unharmed. At the other extreme, older leaves at the extremities of the plant will continue enlarging until they mature, at a size dictated by the distance from other plants and by the time of year.

Planting into the grid pattern

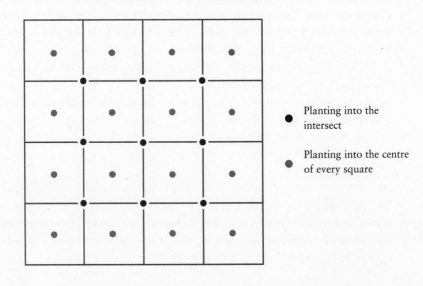

● Planting into the intersect

● Planting into the centre of every square

- The best quality and most viable leaves are those in between the baby ones at the centre and the large, mature, sometimes yellowing, diseased and slug-eaten ones at the edge. My advice is to keep picking the adolescent leaves, at intervals of two or three days to a fortnight from summer to winter, so that plants just keep on growing. Besides the advantage of having less sowing and replanting to do, there will be fewer slugs and healthier leaves, because you are always picking them before they reach their time of decay, which also affords less food and habitat for pests and disease.

- Baby leaves are more tender but are too fiddly to pick individually and are usually obtained by cutting rows of thickly sown seedlings. When doing this, it is difficult to avoid the presence of some yellowing and mildew-infected leaves which occur in densely sown rows, and cutting must be at a height that does not destroy the growing points of the smallest leaves. When using this method, I have found that certain plants live for less long, especially lettuce.

- A third possibility in larger gardens is to have rows with about 7-8cm between plants, and 30-40cm between rows (3" x 15"). The extra spacing allows for repeat cuttings of somewhat larger leaves, as well as allowing better longevity of certain salads such as rocket, chard and mizuna.

STORING AND REVIVING LEAVES

Leaves grown in healthy, fertile soil or compost, and carefully picked when moist, keep remarkably well in cool, damp conditions, such as in a polythene bag at the bottom of the fridge. Basically, they stay alive. A temperature of around 7°C (45°F) is ideal for preserving well-grown leaves in good condition for up to a week if need be. Just be sure to bag up only top quality leaves with no yellowing or mildew.

Should you pick dry, limp leaves, say in a warm afternoon or early evening, place them immediately in cold water so that they can soak up moisture and become firm again. Water is the basis of everything and leaves are nothing without it.

LETTUCE

Until recently lettuce was often the only salad leaf eaten in Britain, and was usually grown into fine, dense hearts. Now we can buy seeds of many other leaves, but lettuce is often still the mainstay of salads because of an increasing range of attractive varieties available and because of its productivity, especially when the outer leaves are repeatedly picked off. Such treatment can keep a window box or container in production for two to three months at a time from the same plants, with a few leaves at each picking. The first leaves are always a little tricky because they lie close to the soil or compost. Be gentle with the plant at this stage, since it is so young and tender. Then each successive picking becomes easier as the lettuce stem gradually thickens and elongates above soil level, like a stumpy little tree. Finally, after up to three months (or much longer for lettuce which have been overwintered under cover) the squat stem will stretch upwards and become a flower stem, at which point its leaves become small and bitter, so the plant should be pulled out and replaced with something different, such as rocket or spinach.

Using this method of picking will provide a regular and quite even supply of leaves over long periods. Nearly all salad plants can be continually cropped like this and a nice benefit is that they grow faster in hot weather, just when you feel like eating more salad. You also need to think ahead and have young plants ready for when existing batches finally rise to seed. A second bed, container or space of some kind is useful for growing on the next batch of plants.

SALAD DAYS FOREVER, IN DIFFERENT SEASONS

For salad days which go on and on:

- Start in late winter or early spring with lettuce, spinach, chard and some herbs, most of which will crop until July.

- Make another sowing in late May, to take over from the first batch in early July. The second sowing can be a mixture of lettuce, chard, summer purslane, basil, and the odd endive.

- In late July you could sow an autumn selection of endives, chicories, rocket, lettuce and various herbs.

- Lastly in late August sow the winter range of rocket, chicories, hardy lettuce, winter purslane, land cress and oriental leaves. See Part Two, pp.68-77 for more details.

Timing of sowings is important in late summer – see later chapters to find precise dates for each kind of leaf. A surprisingly large range of plants lend themselves to production of leaves in the winter season. Although growth is slower and harvests are smaller, flavours are more intense and the pleasure of having your own leaves when they are so rare is a great bonus in itself, apart from the delight of eating them.

SALAD ROTATION

This is not about spinning water out of leaves, but about growing salad of different plant groups in turn, so that different pests and diseases have less chance to accumulate in soil, compost and containers. Lettuce, endive and chicory are all closely related so when they finish it is a good idea to grow any of the brassicas, beet family or herbs and flowers next. Look at the list of plant families below so that, when you have enough space, at least half a year can elapse before members of the same family are grown in the same spot.

Sometimes rotation of crops is not possible, especially where you are filling a restricted area with many kinds of leaf. In small beds or containers it can be more feasible to mix plants up together rather than worry about rotating them in sections. By growing a wide variety of leaves from all families, together with some other vegetables such as baby carrots and beetroot (see Chapter 4) and herbs and flowers, and by following the tips in this book, you should be able to keep growing healthy leaves.

Plant families of salad leaves

Apiaceae/Umbelliferae: carrot, chervil, coriander, dill, fennel, mibuna, parsley, sweet cicely

Asteraceae/Compositae: chicory, endive, lettuce

Brassicaceae/Cruciferae: Chinese cabbage, kale, kohlrabi, land cress, mibuna, mizuna, mustard, pak choi, radish, rape, rocket, tatsoi, turnip, watercress

Chenopodiaceae: beetroot, chard, orache, spinach

Fabaceae/Leguminosae: broad bean, pea

Lamiaceae/Labiatae: basil

Liliaceae: asparagus, chives, garlic, spring onion

Polygonaceae: sorrel

Portulacaceae: purslane

Rosaceae: salad burnet

Valerianaceae: lamb's lettuce

Rotation of salads with other vegetables

The advice on rotation above and in this book generally assumes that salad is the reader's principal and perhaps only vegetable crop.

However, although many vegetables grow too large for the confined spaces covered here, there are some which can be grown in small spaces, before or after crops of salad leaves. I list a few here to give you some ideas: they all grow in half a season, allowing the other half for growing salad.

As an example, you could sow lettuce in late March to harvest through May and June, then grow beetroot as the second crop, see below. Or grow early carrots as below, then plant chicories and endives in late July and up to mid-August, for harvesting in October and November. The first crop can have more time to mature if you raise plants of the second harvest in pots or modules, where they can grow for a month or so before being set in their final position.

- Beetroot: sow March-early April, harvest July or sow early July, harvest October onwards
- Calabrese: sow March (indoors), plant April, harvest July
- Carrots: sow March, harvest June-July or sow July, harvest October-November
- Fennel, bulb: sow July, harvest September-November
- French beans: sow early July, harvest September-October
- Leeks, baby: sow early April, harvest July or sow July, harvest winter
- Onion sets: plant late March, harvest July
- Radish: sow March-April, harvest May-June or sow late July-August, harvest September-November

Chapter 3

Sowing, Planting and Harvesting through the Year

An experiment with salad beds

BRIEF SUMMARY

New beds can be placed on existing surfaces, with no previous preparation. Check below for one or two exceptions.

- *Grass is fine for a base and does not need to be dug or turned over*

- *Sides of 15cm (6") or more can be of wood or plastic: both have advantages and disadvantages*

- *Fill beds with compost, soil and manure according to what is locally available*

- *A range of different plants can be sown or planted to give a continuous and varied mix of leaves*

- *Use the information in other chapters to decide what you will sow and plant at different times of year.*

- *Beds will need regular watering in dry seasons and slug control in wet ones.*

- *The main season of harvest is May to October. Outside this period, leaves grow much more slowly*

- *2-3cm (an inch or so) of fresh compost on top annually will maintain health and fertility*

Salad leaves can be produced continuously from small areas, but how small is small?

It depends on the time of year, how much space you have available...and how many leaves you eat!

To make this clearer, I experimented with and photographed a range of containers, grow-bags and window boxes through the 2007 growing season, to demonstrate some of their relative merits and possibilities. I also looked at the potential of micro leaves, with their small harvests of tender, tasty baby plants – see Chapter 4 for detailed advice on salad in smaller spaces.

A SALAD EXPERIMENT

First off, I created two new beds in late February, one on gravel in our yard and one on grass in the garden. In both instances there was no work on the existing ground surface. I simply created a framework and filled it with organic matter, then sowed and planted straightaway. Plants were picked over and looked after as previously described and yielded leaves over long periods. When each harvest was finished I sowed or planted again with different ones as the seasons changed.

By following the descriptions of what happened in these beds, you will better appreciate the possibilities available and how much time and effort may be needed. Then at the chapter's end is a table of the weekly yields I obtained, from which you can work out how much space you need in relation to the size of beds I used.

ASSEMBLING NEW BEDS

The beds created here were made from old decking wood of 240cm (8') lengths, three pieces per bed. One was cut in half to make the ends of 120cm (4') and I joined the four corners with angle braces, screwed to the insides of the ends of the planks.

In this particular case I sought to recycle some wood, trusting that preservatives will not seep into the soil, but there are other ways of creating beds with untreated wood; for example, some other beds I made were of new softwood which I brushed with two coats of Osmo Wood Protector, a biocide-free wax. This is probably better for the soil but uses new wood and there is currently little information available about whether wood preservatives can leach into soil.

Another idea is to use lengths of link-a-bord plastic, made from recycled pvc. The strips contain air, making them effectively 'double-glazed' and able to better regulate temperature extremes in the beds – cooler in summer and warmer in winter. Also they can be stacked up to make beds of varying heights. However, they are less strong than wood and just 24mm thick compared with the 28mm planks I used. This is a minimum as even my planks showed a tendency to bow outwards on the 240cm sides, but you can anchor the middles firm by driving a peg into the ground where it is soft enough.

FILLING NEW BEDS

- To fill the enclosures I used what came to hand, starting with 5cm (2") of the neighbour's reasonably well rotted horse manure on top of the yard gravel for one bed, and grass for the other. I made a small ramp so that two large wheelbarrow loads could be tipped straight into each bed. This manure holds moisture and slowly releases nutrients as plants require them.

- After levelling it off, I put five wheelbarrow loads of compost made from household recycled waste into each bed, which more than filled them – some treading down was required. This compost had passed through an 8mm sieve before delivery, to remove any wood and plastic.

- Then I spread about 10kg of basalt (volcanic) rock dust over each bed (see *Resources*), my hunch being that this ensures good levels of trace elements in growing plants. It breaks down slowly over many years.

- Lastly I spread one sack of organic multi-purpose compost on top to ensure sufficient nutrients, since, in spite of sieving, the recycled compost contains quite large amounts of tiny pieces of wood, which can absorb nutrients as they continue to decompose. Salads are not heavy feeders but they do need a regular supply of many nutrients.

- The cost of these ingredients was about £9 per bed plus two hours of my time to fetch and spread them. Every household will have different possibilities but the principle of some animal manure on the bottom and finer compost on top is worth aiming for.

- Final smoothing of the compost was done with a small plank of plywood to make the surface even.

- A final touch was to cover the beds with netting to prevent fouling by cats, until plants were established in mid-April.

SOWING, PLANTING AND CROPPING THE BEDS

The beds were finished by late February, too early for first sowings and plantings, but they were ready to use as soon as the weather turned less cold. It transpired that March 2007 was unusually mild so on the 10th I planted some module-grown lettuce, spinach, chard and coriander which had been sown eight weeks earlier in the greenhouse, and sowed more of the same directly in the surface of the beds, as well as some peas (see opposite).

A week later I set out plants of komatsuna, turnip greens, ruby mustard and rocket. These are marginal for spring use because their leaves are often holed by flea beetles and they crop for only a short time before flowering – the plants in this case were finished by early May. However, any salad in early spring is welcome and they bring different flavours.

The real stars in spring salads are lettuce, the main ingredient of my first harvest on 14th April, which weighed in at 0.5kg per bed. By the following week the quantity had doubled and it stayed thereabouts until early June, with a range of ingredients reflecting the initial sowings, and lettuce comprising about three quarters of the total.

More sowings and plantings were made after plants had run to seed and been removed to the compost heap. The table opposite lists all sowings and planting for a whole season's cropping and is to give you ideas; bear in mind that it covers both beds and so half the plantings and clearings would be needed for just one bed.

Leaves can be gathered when it is convenient: every day, twice weekly or weekly, although any longer than weekly will see them become rather large. When picked damp in the early morning, late evening or after rain, and washed in cold water, they will remain crisp and firm for many days – say in a polythene bag kept in the bottom of a fridge.

WATERING

Large volumes of compost can hold plenty of moisture, more than ordinary soil, so a thorough watering once weekly should be sufficient in dry weather. For a bed of 240 x 120cm you will need 30-50 litres (7-11 gallons) of water each time, and every three days or so in the hottest weather. It is better to water gently out of a can with a rose than with a jet of water from a hose, so that water has time to dampen the compost and soak in, rather than running off.

In the summer half of the year, after a few days of sun or warm winds, the sides of raised beds become especially dry and need extra water. Ants often invade any warm, dry spots so it is worth keeping the sides as moist as possible. Recycled plastic is better than wood in this respect, or you can line the wooden sides with polythene.

SLUGS

Some seasons see enough rain that watering is scarcely necessary, but then slugs require attention instead. On damp evenings from late June to late August 2007, when rainfall peaked, I regularly discovered slugs heading for the salad bed. I have tried many of the more commonly suggested remedies (see Chapter 8, pp.60-65 for help with these) and find that in seasons of excessive moisture, dusk or dawn patrols to kill them are invaluable.

An advantage of planting at wider spacings and picking leaves regularly is that slugs have less or no hiding place, so there should not be any living on the bed surface except when you grow larger, hearting salads.

WEEKLY SOWINGS, PLANTINGS AND CLEARINGS ON BOTH BEDS

This table is a reflection of my aim to grow many different leaves on two separate beds, to always fill every gap that arose and to keep the beds cropping through winter. It could be simplified by choosing to grow fewer kinds of leaves and leaving occasional bare patches instead.

By using the table for the length of harvest period and my remarks, and information about different plants in the rest of this book, you can imagine roughly what you could be eating when.

Seed was sown into the modules in a greenhouse for later planting in the bed, unless the plant name is followed by (s), when it was sown directly into the bed.

Date	Planted	Harvest Period	Remarks
10 Mar	Lettuce, 6 varieties*	11 Apr–early July	Consistent, bulky harvests
	Spinach *Tarpy*	14 Apr–19 May	Final large picking to cook
	Spinach *Regiment*	18 Apr–15 Jun	Smaller picks but longer season
	Chard ruby and yellow	14 Apr–15 Nov	Flowering stems pinched out
	Beet *Red Titan*	14 Apr–8 Nov	Small, dense, rich colour
	Coriander, *Confetti*	18 Apr–19 Jun	Flowering by mid-May
	Spinach *Tetona* (s)	18 Apr–22 Jun	Dark, round leaves
	Chard ruby and yellow (s)	18 Apr–15 Nov	Almost too productive
	Lettuce, 6 varieties (s)	25 Apr–mid-July	Cut, then massively thinned
	Pea *Ambassador* (s)	18 Apr–12 July	Fleshiest shoots in May
16 Mar	Komatsuna	18 Apr–8 May	Some slug damage
	Turnip greens	18 Apr–8 May	Aphids and virus in May
	Ruby mustard	25 Apr–8 May	Aphids meant small harvest
	Rocket	18 Apr–15 May	Aphids meant small harvest
22 Mar	Spring onion *White Lisbon*	28 Apr–19 Jun	Each clump made a bunch

Date	Planted	Harvest Period	Remarks
28 Mar	Sorrel, broad-leaved	8 May–6 Dec	Many small, tasty harvests
	Red-ribbed dandelion	8 May–29 Nov	Flowering stems pinched out
1 May	Orach (s)	19 May–11 Jul	Small dark leaves
19 Jun	Endive yellow leaf	13 Jul–6 Dec	Pretty leaves every week
	Lettuce, 5 varieties**	13 Jul–21 Sep	Consistent growth
	Parsley, curly and plain	20 Jul–13 Dec	Still healthy at year's end
	Radicchio *Palla Rossa*	17-29 Aug + Oct	Hearts first then re-growth
	Purslane, Green	Failed	Disliked wet summer
27 Jul	Mustards, Ruby and Golden	10 Aug–15 Nov	For autumn not winter leaves
	Leaf radish	10 Aug–26 Oct	For autumn not winter leaves
	Spinach *Tetona* (s)	24 Aug–1 Nov	Some slug holes
	Rocket (s)	24 Aug–6 Dec	Variable quality, steady growth
	Mizuna (s)	17 Aug–5 Oct	Rapid to start and to flower
30 Jul	Leaf chicory, 10 varieties***(s)	31 Aug–20 Dec	Leaves smaller by December
8 Aug	Lettuce, 4 varieties****	31 Aug–13 Dec	Grenoble Red lasted longest
	Pak Choi, *Joi Choi*	31 Aug–5 Oct	Many slug holes
31 Aug	Lamb's Lettuce, *D'Orlanda*	8 Nov–27 Mar	Small, high quality harvests
7 Sep	Mustard, *Golden Streaks*	5 Oct–6 Dec	Feathery leaves, strong taste
	Tatsoi	5 Oct–8 Nov	Mostly slug-holed
14 Sep	Mizuna	5 Oct–6 Dec	Some fungal diseases later
	Kohlrabi, purple-leaved	19 Oct–20 Dec	Small pickings
	Rocket, Salad	5 Oct–20 Dec	Good growth in late autumn
	Lamb's Lettuce (s)	5 Feb–mid-Apr	Welcome leaves in late winter

* March lettuce varieties: **Grenoble Red, Bijou, Bergamo, Bridgemere, Catalogna, Mottistone**

** June lettuce varieties: **Foxley, Bridgemere, Chartwell, Mottistone, Redina**

*** July leaf chicories: all those listed on p.114

**** August lettuce varieties: **Grenoble Red, Appleby, Rosemoor, Chartwell**

WEEKLY TOTAL OF LEAVES (TWO BEDS 1.2m x 2.4m), AND WEATHER NOTES

I include the notes on weather because it affects speed and quality of growth so much. 2007 was characterised in Somerset by unusual warmth in spring, unusual rainfall in summer and an unusually fine autumn. All three caused extra salad to grow, as long as slugs were kept under control. So yields might be a little lower in other years.

Date Amount Remarks

Date	Amount	Remarks
14 Apr	1.0kg	Mostly lettuce, earlier than usual
21 Apr	2.1kg	Unseasonable warmth, even a few pea shoots
25 Apr	1.9kg	Plenty of chard and coriander
1 May	2.0kg	Still so warm, flea beetle holes in rocket, mustard, turnip greens
8 May	2.3kg	Hot weather, unusually large harvests
15 May	2.2kg	Rain at last
24 May	3.1kg	Leaves increasing in size and thickness, weather cooler
1 Jun	3.9kg	Large harvest, enough for half a dozen hungry households
8 Jun	4.8kg	Serious surplus! Warm, moist weather
15 Jun	4.4kg	Less spinach
22 Jun	3.9kg	Lettuce slowing down with smaller leaves
29 Jun	3.5kg	Thinner pea shoots
6 Jul	2.8kg	Spring flush is over, some lettuce is flowering
13 Jul	3.1kg	Fleshy leaves in damp weather, slug patrols every night
20 Jul	2.5kg	Leaves harvested in torrential rain, good quality, last of early lettuce
27 Jul	2.2kg	Slight lull and no purslane
3 Aug	2.3kg	More sun is helping growth
10 Aug	2.4kg	New lettuce now producing, also mustard and leaf radish
17 Aug	1.9kg	More cool rain, first radicchio heart
24 Aug	1.6kg	Growth slowed by cool, cloudy weather, still squashing slugs
29 Aug	1.9kg	Extra harvest of four radicchio hearts – keep well in fridge
31 Aug	2.5kg	Return of sunshine, healthy lettuce and first chicory leaves
7 Sep	2.3kg	Mix includes lettuce, spinach, rocket, mustards, endive, chicory, sorrel
14 Sep	2.1kg	Leaves still plentiful
21 Sep	1.2kg	Suddenly growth has slowed and some lettuce have flowered
28 Sep	0.4kg	Cool autumn mornings, smaller leaves on all plants
5 Oct	1.1kg	Milder weather, a welcome boost to growth
12 Oct	1.1kg	Still a lovely varied mix of many leaves
19 Oct	1.2kg	Warm sun has boosted growth
26 Oct	0.4kg	Leaves markedly smaller in reducing daylight
1 Nov	0.4kg	Small leaves – still numerous
8 Nov	0.4kg	Harvest boosted by the first lamb's lettuce
15 Nov	0.2kg	First frost has reduced new growth
22 Nov	0.3kg	Small radicchio heart increased the harvest
29 Nov	0.3kg	Same as last week, mix of lamb's lettuce, chicories, rocket, bits and pieces
6 Dec	0.4kg	Excellent yield after mild weather
13 Dec	0.8kg	Last, large heart of radicchio, beautiful leaves
20 Dec	0.3kg	Frosty: Christmas salad of lamb's lettuce, chicory, rocket, chard, mustard

TOTAL 71.2kg, equating to 470 salad packs of 150g, and varied harvests of different flavours every week. Small harvests continued through the winter as this book was going to press

These quantities are more than most families or households would require, so you can make smaller beds in proportion to what you eat. But remember that to have enough, you need to grow too much, because growing is affected by unforeseeable events and is not programmable. In times of glut, enjoy giving some fine leaves to friends and neighbours.

Also from late September the weekly harvests are much lower, so at this time of year a larger bed is advantageous. Summer gluts can be avoided by, for example, growing some onions, carrots or early French beans at one end of a large bed. When they finish in early August, there is still time to sow rocket, mustards, kale, chicories, endives, winter purslane and so forth, to ensure enough leaves when the weather cools down.

Alternatively take a look at the next chapter for ideas on growing smaller leaves in smaller spaces.

Chapter 4

Small Spaces and Micro Leaves

Growing in confined areas
and picking baby leaves

BRIEF SUMMARY

- *Large containers allow long-term, regular cropping of many leaf types*
- *Window boxes are more suited to baby or very small leaves and need more regular watering*
- *Grow-bags are more difficult because they offer sanctuary to slugs*
- *Slugs need careful surveillance in container salad growing; I offer tips for reducing their damage, but there are no certain remedies*
- *Baby leaves can be grown in trays or beds of shallow compost*

This chapter describes growing salad in containers, window boxes and grow-bags. It also explains the growing and harvesting of baby salads, sometimes called micro or living leaves.

SUITABLE CONTAINERS AND WINDOW BOXES

The more compost you can fit in a container, the longer you will be able to crop your salad and the larger the leaves will be. I have had good crops from round terracotta pots of 60cm (24") diameter, old plastic bath tubs with holes cut in the bottom, square 40cm (16") wide terracotta pots, and a range of window boxes of different sizes and materials.

A major constraint in container growing is the need to water frequently, so terracotta, which breathes moisture from the compost and out to the atmosphere, is less desirable although it looks lovely. Glazed pots are better in this respect and you can also line the insides of clay containers with polythene, especially the sides of small terracotta window boxes.

Plastic containers obviously do not have this problem and are much lighter to move around. But since plastic conducts heat more quickly than clay, roots may be (but in practice rarely are) damaged by heat in summer and frost in winter. A solution for this is 'double-glazed', recycled plastic window boxes whose layer of air between the PVC sides acts as a heat buffer (see *Resources*).

I hesitate to recommend plastic because of its dubious pedigree and afterlife, but sheer durability makes it a reasonably ecological choice, as plastic containers can be re-used so many times. Also I never wash or sterilise mine when refilling and their crops have always been as good as those in terracotta.

SLUGS

Never underestimate the extent of this problem! One large slug can eat plenty of salad leaves while you are asleep, which is why I recommend pots rather than grow-bags – their moist plastic affords a perfect resting-place to slugs and snails. Keep grow-bags for tomatoes and other tall summer crops.

Unless you want to use chemical poisons to control slugs – and I am certainly not recommending them – vigilance is vital.

Here are some golden rules for reasonable long-term peace of mind:

- Place containers as far as you can from walls and clumps of thick vegetation, and in as full sunlight as possible
- Take a wander at dawn and dusk before planting to squash or remove any molluscs
- Have a little rummage under nearby leaves and stones to remove what is lurking
- Water in the morning so surface moisture has evaporated by nightfall

Here are some less effective controls, worth trying but not guaranteed to be totally successful. Their limitation, apart from the nematodes, is that slugs are only ever deterred rather than reduced in number:

Copper strips around containers keep most slugs at bay, as long as you ensure there are no leaves overhanging the sides; apparently the copper gives a small electric shock to slimy pests.

Organic slug gel and pellets, salt, soot, wood ash etc. may limit the damage, but are not foolproof and their overuse may poison the growing medium.

Slug nematodes will offer protection but only for about six weeks and they are expensive.

COMPOST

A good compost is the key to abundant, healthy crops. I can offer limited advice here since commercial composts are changing all the time, especially organic ones that are more difficult to create to a constant formula. As an example, I have enjoyed success with West Riding Organics' module compost which is based on screenings from reservoirs in the Yorkshire Moors. Quality and quantity of growth are excellent and it's only drawback is a number of seeds of sedge grasses, which I mention to make the point that there is probably no perfect organic compost!

PLANT SPACINGS

Salad plants can be grown a little closer in containers than in beds for a greater variety of leaves, as long as they are picked over regularly to keep leaf growth in balance with more restricted root runs. Or, if you want fewer and larger leaves, I recommend using the suggested spacings in Part Three.

LIQUID FEEDING (OR NOT) AND REJUVENATING COMPOST

Salads are less greedy than tomatoes and I rarely give them liquid feed. New compost should grow leaves for a few months without extra nutrients. After a crop finishes, one way of rejuvenating compost is to incorporate some dried comfrey and alfalfa pellets before replanting (see *Resources*). Treated in this way, I have containers with three-year-old compost that are still growing healthy plants, which have included tomatoes and courgettes.

WATERING

Moisture levels in container compost can be difficult to gauge and in wet weather they can look damp enough yet be dry underneath. Remember that plants are pumping moisture from a limited volume and sometimes it is good to lift containers gently to check that they are still heavy and full of moisture. Using a saucer under small pots will give you an idea if water has flowed to the bottom, but watch out that saucers do not cause waterlogging in extremely wet weather and remove them in winter.

INFLUENCE OF LIGHT LEVELS

Containers are often placed in part shade and overlooked by walls, while window boxes, unless they are south-facing, receive only half-light. This makes quite a difference to the vigour of the plants. So choose the sunniest or lightest spot you can find and you should then be pleased with the results of your labours.

CROPPING EXAMPLES – LEAVES FROM POTS

Below are some examples of salad leaves and vegetables grown by me in containers to give you an idea of possible sowings, plantings and harvests, as well as what kind of second crops to grow after the first ones finish in midsummer.

All pots and boxes were filled with West Riding Organics' multipurpose compost and no liquid feed was given at all. A little extra compost or nutrients were added before replanting. The only slug defence in a wet summer was regular patrols at dawn and dusk to catch several of them before damage occurred.

Leaf lettuce and carrots in a large terracotta container

In a round terracotta container measuring 63cm (25") in diameter and holding forty litres of compost, I planted thirteen lettuce plants on 10 March, from a mid-January indoor sowing. These were *Grenoble Red, Mottistone, Bergamo, Catalogna, Solstice* and *Bridgemere* for a range of leaf shape and colour.

They were picked weekly from mid-April, yielding leaves about 60% of the size of bed-grown lettuce. The *Solstice* rose to flower in mid-June but the other twelve plants were still producing leaves until late July, making a worthwhile harvest over three and a half months.

To follow them I mixed some lucerne pellets into the compost and sowed *Mini Finger* patio carrots in early August which cropped from late October until after Christmas as there was nothing more than light frost. The largest carrots were, as their name suggests, the size of little fingers and of excellent flavour – delicious in winter salad. Carrots are a useful crop in terms of rotation, to give containers a rest from growing leaves (see Chapter 2).

Another option, of which there are many in early August, would have been to sow or plant any or all of rocket, winter purslane, spinach, endive and oriental leaves such as mizuna, pak choi and mustard.

Leaf lettuce and chicories in a window box

In a plastic window box measuring 48cm x 23cm (19" x 9"), I planted one plant each of *Grenoble Red*, *Freckles*, *Bergamo* and *Bijou* in early April. They cropped from late April until late July, about ten medium-sized leaves per week on average. The plants were kept small by frequent harvesting: this helped reduce the need to water.

I uprooted the flowering stems and then pretended to be on holiday until 22nd August when I re-planted the window box with three leaf chicories and an endive, harvesting a few small leaves in early September and then about eight to ten weekly through October, and half that through the winter.

Basil and rocket in terracotta window boxes

In a terracotta window box measuring 31cm x 16cm (12" x 6"), I set out two red basil plants in late June, and enjoyed small pickings through the summer, which was a cool season and not beneficial to basil. Last pickings were in early October. In another similar box I planted two *Skyrocket* on 22nd August and it took only ten days for them to produce a few small leaves. Harvests were steady through September, a little smaller in October and occasional thereafter. I did not line the terracotta with plastic, so needed to water regularly, even in midwinter.

Mixed salad leaves in a window box

On 20th June in a Link-a-Bord window box measuring 210 x 110cm (7' x 3'6"), I planted one each of red basil, *Nufari* green basil, curled parsley, three lettuces – *Grenoble Red*, *Freckles* and *Mottistone*, and two endives – *Bianca Riccia da Taglio* and *Fine de Louviers*. Leaves were gathered from early July, occasionally quite large handfuls. The lettuce was starting to flower by late August so I removed it and planted baby leaf kohlrabi, *Fairway* rocket and sowed red-stemmed leaf radish on 27 August.

By about 8th September it was apparent that the large parsley and endive plants were rooting more powerfully than the young salads and depriving them of nutrients, so although they were still cropping well I twisted them out and planted mizuna, *Apollo* rocket, red-stemmed leaf radish and tatsoi instead, to have all young plants of the same size growing together. First leaves picked on 18th October were about 80g in weight, thereafter pickings were somewhat less although consistent – for garnish more than a large meal.

Beetroot then leaf lettuce in a terracotta pot

In a 36cm (14") diameter pot I planted module-raised *Boltardy* beetroot in late April, yielding 620g of sweet, baby roots by early July. On 14th July I planted four lettuces – *Grenoble Red, Maravilla di Verano, Nymans* and *Roselee* – of which the last was eaten by slugs – and subsequently picked leaves weekly until early November. The highest harvest was 170g on August 29th.

BABY LEAVES (ALSO CALLED 'MICRO' LEAVES AND 'LIVING' LEAVES)

For the quickest results and in the smallest of spaces, you can grow seedling salad, either by cutting whole baby plants or by harvesting their tiny leaves. Less compost is needed to grow them, and sowing to harvest is less than three weeks for brassicas in summer. Two seed trays on the window sill, alternately sown and harvested, could keep you in a sprinkling of saladings from late April until November.

Greenhouse micro-leaf bed 1.2m x 1.05m (4' x 3'6")

To explore the possibilities of different leaves, I created a bed in the greenhouse on top of a pallet, just over a metre square and lined with old fleece. Sides were made by screwing some old 15cm (6") planks to the pallet's edges. After firming the 6cm (2") of multi-purpose compost gently, I marked 15cm intervals along all the sides and then ran a small bamboo between them, across the top of the compost, to mark out a grid pattern of fifty-six 15cm squares.

First sowing

On 6th August I sowed different seeds in each square, except for twelve that were sown three days later when more seeds arrived in the post. It is hard to sow precisely and a few squares had over fifty seeds in. A week later I realised that some seed was too thickly sown, so I thinned out baby seedlings to a spacing of about one plant every 2cm (1") – about thirty plants per 15cm square.

Just over two weeks later, in thinning out the too-thick sowings, I harvested a bowl of wonderfully varied baby plants, comprising a huge range of tastes, by cutting them just above the compost with an extremely sharp knife. Careful cutting avoids any uprooting of seedlings and can mean the leaves do not need washing, while a layer of vermiculite on top of the compost is an optional extra to help the harvest stay clean.

By 25th August the bed was groaning with leaves, especially its twenty-four members of the fast-growing cabbage family. 600g was harvested and I should have picked more but our appetites could not keep up with the new growth. On September 3rd I cut 1.2kg of rather larger leaves for the local pub, then another 700g of re-growth a week later. By this stage many plants had been cut close to or below their growing point of smallest leaves, meaning that subsequent harvests were becoming smaller and harder to gather amongst the increasing number of older, yellowing leaves. So I pulled out all stems and roots, shaking off any loose compost before starting again.

Second sowing

The bed was replenished with another 1cm (½") of compost and re-sown from late September for autumn leaves. There were four leaves on most plants by 29 October when I picked and cut a small bucketful of baby leaves, 550g in weight, from the faster-growing plants such as leaf radish, mustard, rocket, mizuna and mibuna.

Small pickings were then taken every week in November, between 110-150g of baby leaves, mostly cut. Growth thereafter was slower but plants stayed healthy and offered occasional small leaves. I tend to cut across the top where close growth has resulted in many tiny leaves – often the case with mustards and mizuna – or pick leaf by leaf where they are larger, often possible with leaf radish and *Apollo* rocket.

By mid-December some lower leaves were yellow and the bed was running low in nutrients. A liquid feed is called for at this point and I used Ocean Grown seawater for a mineral-rich range of nutrients (see *Resources*). This experiment resulted in the following advice:

Tips on growing baby leaves

- For continuous supply, EITHER sow little and often – say every two to three weeks, and cut young plants at stem level, OR grow in a larger, slightly deeper bed or container and harvest carefully (above the growing point).
- Cutting baby plants at stem level means immediate re-sowing, whereas allowing them to grow a little more and picking or cutting some of their baby leaves will allow another small harvest.
- Stems of baby plants have juicy sap of appealing flavour.
- Some unusual flavours include carrot tops, red cabbage, lovage, radish, fennel and Mesembryanthemum. Any plant listed in Chapter 5 can be used.

- Flavours of baby leaves are true to type, subtly different and milder than flavours of larger leaves.

Special tips for seedlings in seed trays

- Seed trays work well in small areas for growing selections of baby leaves. Fill them to about three-quarters depth with multi-purpose compost. Two or three harvests is a reasonable target.

- Cress and brassicas (mizuna, rocket, mustards, cabbages, kales etc), as well as being the quickest, are the easiest to harvest.

- Most thickly sown carpets of seedlings need cutting before the first true leaves are fully grown; otherwise there may be a lot of yellowing cotyledons in the harvest. Sow more thinly if you want plants to grow their true leaves.

- Red amaranth is an excellent plant for some vivid colour in Summer and Autumn

- Old mushroom boxes, which are deeper than seed trays, can be lined with cardboard or polythene, filled with compost and sown a little more thinly – say one plant every 2.5cm (1") – for repeated picking of small leaves.

Chapter 5

Leaf Flavours

An amazing palette to choose from

BRIEF SUMMARY

- *Certain groups of leaves share many taste characteristics*

- *The large cabbage family is characterised by a spicy, mustard character, more pronounced as leaves grow larger and older*

- *Chicories and endives possess a range of flavours but are all more or less bitter, especially as leaves rather than hearts*

- *Plants of spinach and beets have strongly flavoured and rather metallic-tasting leaves*

- *Many herbs are mild enough to enjoy with salad leaves, and there is a huge range of flavours*

- *There is a most interesting group of other leaves which boasts some appealing tastes such as pea shoots, purslane and lambs lettuce*

The tasting notes below will, I hope, help point you towards those leaves you most enjoy – there are certainly plenty to choose from.

The table overleaf gives an overall picture of the depth and quality of flavour of different leaves. Pungency is to the right, other elements of taste such as aroma, bitterness and acidity are towards the bottom. For example, *Green in the Snow* mustard is the hottest leaf here and sorrel is the most acid, while lamb's lettuce is the mildest, in my opinion!

LEAF FLAVOURS

Mild Flavour (mildest at top)	*Some heat*	*Hot mustard*
Lamb's lettuce, Chinese cabbage		
Lettuce	Leaf radish	
Purslane	Pak choi	Rocket
Pea shoots, Mizuna, Red Russian kale	Komatsuna, Mibuna	*Ruby Streaks*
Mitsuba, Spinach, Chards(A), Tatsoi		*Golden Streaks*
Endives, Chicories(B)		*Red Giant*
Parsley		*Green in the Snow*
Chervil		Cress
Basil	Dill	Coriander
Sorrel(A)		

Key: A = Acid, B = Bitter

DESCRIPTIONS OF LEAVES FROM 3-4 WEEK OLD PLANTS

BRASSICAS (CABBAGE FAMILY)

Chinese broccoli *Kailaan*
Tall-growing, mild and juicy with a slight mustard flavour.

Chinese broccoli *Nabana*
Slightly hairy, large, tender leaves with mild flavour and pale green stems.

Chinese cabbage *Kiansi*
Large rounded leaves, thick and slightly hairy with a succulent, mild watery flavour. By a month old it also has crunchy, tasty, white stems.

Kale *Nero di Toscana* (also called *Black Cabbage*)
Dark and thin, somewhat spicy and pungent.

Kale *Red Russian*
Mild flavour and, unlike most other kales, leaves are tender and smooth, with pretty mauve and feathery leaves.

Kohlrabi *Purple-leaved*
Its leaves actually taste of kohlrabi, rooty and turnip-like in a pleasing way.

Komatsuna *Mustard Spinach*
Long-stemmed and oval-shaped, of cabbage flavour but extremely mild and watery when young. Slightly crunchy.

Mibuna *Mibuna*
Thin-leaved and tender, with a certain pungency which increases as the leaves rapidly grow larger.

Mizuna *Kyoto*
Feathery leaves are tender, mild, soft and watery with long white stems.

Mizuna *Namenia*
Juicy and watery, slightly mustard-like, with quite large leaves.

Mizuna *Sessantina*
A larger-leaved and similar-tasting mizuna, crunchy-stemmed and mild with just a hint of cabbage in young leaves.

Mustard *Golden Streaks*
Bright green and feathery, juicy and mild initially but with a hot aftertaste.

Mustard *Green in the Snow*
Hot and spicy as a small leaf, becomes extremely pungent as it matures.

Mustard *Red Giant*
Hot, even when small-leaved, more green than red in warm weather.

Mustard *Ruby Streaks*
Agreeable and bittersweet, followed by a hot aftertaste. Colour becomes more ruby in cold weather.

Pak choi *Hanakan*
Mild and crunchy, especially its thick white stem.

Pak choi *Sai Sai*
Has thinner stems, longer leaves and a similar gentle cabbage flavour.

Radish *French Breakfast*
Slightly hairy, mild radish flavour.

Radish leaf *Sai Sai*
Smoother and larger than *French Breakfast*, pleasantly mild, a hint of radish to taste and a faintly hot aftertaste.

Rape *Fodder Rape Salad*
Tender and tasting like mizuna, an agreeable flavour and fast-growing.

Red Cabbage
More tender, sweeter and milder than larger cabbage leaves.

Rocket *Salad*
Mild as a baby leaf, quickly heating up as it grows, often a little sweet.

Rocket *Skyrocket*
The normal rocket flavour, reasonably mild on aftertaste too.

Rocket *Wild*
More pungent than salad rocket with much thinner leaves.

Tatsoi *Tah Sai*
Compact crunchy plants, pretty, mild and watery with a slightly aromatic flavour.

Tatsoi *Yukina Savoy*
A tatsoi of mild flavour but a little more chewy than Tah Sai and a tannic aftertaste.

Texel greens
Mild and sweet, similar size and appearance to rape – oval-shaped, slightly waxy, mid-green leaves.

Turnip
The young leaves are mild and tender, with gentle turnip flavour.

SPINACH/CHARD/BEET

Beetroot *Boltardy* and *Vulkan Red Beet*
A strong taste of beetroot, pungent, a few leaves go a long way.

Chard *Rainbow*
Lightly tannic and acid, of metallic flavour; best eaten with other leaves.

Spinach *Campania and Oriento*
Tender leaves and juicy, slightly sweet, flavours of iron and tannin, piquant aftertaste.

CHICORIES, ENDIVES

Chicory *Catalogna*
Thin and tender, more bitter than sweet, balanced by slight acidity.

Chicory *Da Taglio Bionda*
Markedly bitter and best used in small amounts, with thin smooth leaves.

Chicory *Treviso Svelta*
Prettily speckled, bitter-sweet and tender, with long thick-stemmed leaves.

Chicory *Zuccherina di Trieste*
Not as sweet as its name suggests!

Dandelion *Red-ribbed*
Long and thin, rather acid and bitter but full of flavour.

Endive *Bianca Riccia Da Taglio*
Pale yellow, tender and mildly bitter-sweet.

Endive *Romanesco*
Fuller flavour than the chicories, slightly less bitter with long serrated leaves.

HERBS

Burnet *Salad*
Small, tough, slightly bitter and tannic, like eating paper I imagine.

Chervil *Plain*
Mild and minty with a taste that lingers agreeably.

Coriander *Bilbo*
Rather aggressive, a full coriander flavour. Pungent.

Dill *Dukat*
Compact, feathery leaves and a mild, minty flavour, different from mature leaves which pack more punch and have a sharp bite.

Fennel *Common*
When small and tender offers a full fennel flavour, slightly more pungent as it matures.

Lovage (*no named variety*)
Bittersweet and many layers of flavour, great range of aromatic tastes, impressive.

Parsley *Moss Curled*
A slightly stronger, more pungent flavour than plain- or flat-leaved, with a sweet aftertaste.

Parsley *Plain-leaved*
Mild and slightly acid with aromatic hints of fragrant drying grass.

Sorrel *Broad-leaved*
Full of rich lemon flavours, slightly acid and mouth tingling.

Sorrel *Buckler-leaved*
Small tender leaves with fantastic mouth-filling taste of lemon, with a juicy acidity.

BABY LEAVES OF ROOT VEGETABLES

Beetroot – see page 42.

Carrot *Early Nantes*
Lovely hint of sweetness to a quite deep flavour of carrot, slightly acid.

Fennel Bulb *Montebianco*
Feathery leaves with intriguing minty, aniseed flavours.

Parsnip *White Gem*
Pungent baby leaves, unmistakeable flavour of parsnip and a rather bitter aftertaste.

OTHER

Amaranth *Garnet Red*
Handsome tiny and dark red leaves with some variegations. Chewy with a grassy flavour, rather dull and flat.

Chenopodium *Tree spinach*
Tastes more like Mesembryanthemum than spinach, very mild.

Cress *Cressida*
Tall and spindly with a hot, spicy taste and lingering aromas.

Japanese parsley *Mitsuba*
Notably herby with hints of parsley, celery and other herbs combining in a subtle way.

Lamb's lettuce *D'Orlanda*
Mild, firm-textured and slightly waxy.

Lettuce *Grenoble Red*
Gentle aromatic flavour, slightly bitter and tannic, no powerful aftertastes. Most lettuces have consistently mild flavours, with only small varietal difference. **Batavians** such as *Maravilla de Verano (Canasta)* and *Grenoble Red* are perhaps the most tasty; whole-hearted lettuce such as *Little Gem* and *Lobjoits* are sweet as well.

Mesembryanthemum *Magic Carpet*
Pretty reddish stems, so soft they almost melt in the mouth, watery and fresh with a hint of acidity.

Pea *Ambassador*
Juicy and of rich pea flavour, with short and dark green shoots.

Pea *Tall Sugar*
Longer and paler shoots, a little sweeter, tender and succulent. The pea flavours are really delicious.

Purslane *Green*
Pretty and juicy with a crunchy stem and pleasant citric tang which explodes in a mild way as one bites into it.

GLOSSARY OF TERMS

- **Acid** equates to tangy, sharp, clean and sour. These slightly derogatory terms are misleading because small doses of clean acidity are refreshing and contribute to the balance of other tastes when used in the right proportion.

- **Aftertaste** is the sensation of flavour which lingers when food has been swallowed, and it may reveal different flavours from those experienced when food is still in the mouth.

- **Citric** is a description of certain acid tastes which are most commonly found in lemons and limes.

- **Pungent**, mustardy tastes can be aggressively dominant and need respect. They often surface as hot aftertastes behind other, milder flavours which have expressed themselves, and they may linger for a time in the mouth.

- **Sour** – see acid above.

- **Sweet tastes** are rare but welcome in salad leaves, especially when they balance the bitterness of chicories and endives. They are most common in hearts and can be augmented by blanching any leaves, excluding all light for a week or so.

FLAVOUR CHANGES WITH MATURITY

The mildest flavours are found in young, small leaves, and even the first cotyledons of certain herbs, such as lovage, are packed full of taste and aroma.

The development of flavour as leaves grow and plants mature is to be welcomed if you like stronger flavours, and is especially pronounced in the cabbage family. Baby rocket leaves are utterly different from large ones, and also from small leaves of older rocket plants which can be surprisingly hot. If you want mild flavours of certain fast-growing brassica salads, you need to pick them frequently to keep leaves small, especially in warm weather, and to re-sow at intervals.

The other way in which maturity affects flavour is the sweetening of leaves in hearting plants. Sweetness is the least common element of taste found in salad leaves but the pale hearts of lettuce, endive and chicory have enough sugars to create a wonderful balance and depth of flavour.

FLAVOUR CHANGES WITH SEASON

It is intriguing that each season clearly defines the flavours of salad leaves, when plants are grown at their best time. There are two elements to this:

Firstly, the flavours of some leaves change with the seasons. Cold weather, for instance, has a sweetening effect on many endives and chicories. In addition it can happen that we perceive flavours differently as our bodies adapt to changing weather and day length.

Secondly, each season has a characteristic, overall flavour of its own leaves. Spring shows the greatest variety and rhythm of change as strong tasting winter leaves make way for more subtle and fragrant new ones. The dominance of lettuce in late spring and summer makes for a quiet background flavour which is punctuated by some exciting aromas of herbs and other plants. Autumn then brings much stronger flavours as brassicas, chicories and endives arrive in season. Both pungency and bitterness are then freely available and they become stronger in winter as leaf size and wateriness are reduced. I do wonder if the powerful flavours of winter leaves are a reflection of their ability to help our bodies withstand periods of cold and darkness. The arrival of fragrant new growth in spring is then a wake-up call, bringing new energy and vitality.

Take a look at Part Two for information on the best times to sow all these different leaves and a fuller idea of how to create your favourite seasonal salads.

Chapter 6

Sowing, Raising, Sustaining

Healthy plants, indoors and outside

BRIEF SUMMARY

- *Outdoor sowing is more weather-dependent than indoor sowing*

- *Seed of different salads in each season can be sown outdoors from about mid-March to mid-September*

- *Indoor sowings can be done in a variety of covered spaces, preferably with full daylight*

- *There is a variety of growing media, compost and sowing techniques*

- *Growing in modules gives reliable plants which transplant easily*

- *Diseases of small plants are rare, but slugs need careful surveillance*

Early growth from seed is tender and often slow, so a plant's first tiny leaves are vulnerable to grazing by slugs and, since they are so small, it often takes just one nibble for the whole plant to disappear. Such disappearances are often blamed on poor germination but close examination may reveal a few thin, pale stalks.

Because of this, it is often more reliable to raise plants in a protected environment before setting them out in beds or pots. Also, more cropping time is gained by not having to wait for plants to grow *in situ* from seed. This is explained in detail on pp.51-3.

SOWING OUTDOORS

If you have no indoor facilities, look carefully at this section for guidelines on which outdoor sowings work best and in which season. For example, spinach and chard in the spring and oriental leaves in late summer often work well from direct sowing.

The timing of your first outdoor sowings is never written in stone because it depends on many variable factors:

Weather varies from spring to spring and can postpone first sowing by two or three weeks. March is the month when one starts looking for opportunities, but stormy conditions with lashings of cold rain, or regular frost at night, invite a wait for better weather. On average in most of Britain I recommend first sowings between about 10th March and 10th April, depending also on your plot.

Soil conditions play a major role. If your allotment or garden has a poorly drained clay soil which lies wet, it will take much longer to warm up and enable seedlings to grow than, for example, the test beds and containers featured in Chapters 3 and 4. Their soft, friable compost allows free passage of any heavy rain and the dark colour of compost is quicker than a light-coloured soil to heat up in any sun. This makes growth earlier, stronger and more likely to survive any slug attacks.

The situation of growing media must also be considered. If containers or your garden are mostly shaded from the spring sun, I recommend sowing a week or two later.

These observations relate to dates of sowings in early spring and late autumn only. Sowing dates in summer and early autumn are mostly governed by day length, as opposed to weather, and do not vary from year to year.

Also remember that spring sowings tend to 'catch up'. A mid-March sowing of spinach which suffers cold winds and rain may crop only a little before an early April sowing which enjoyed steady warmth. The variability of weather brings an element of uncertainty to all early and late sowing dates.

If you are interested in considering the effects of the moon when working out your sowing dates have a look at Chapter 7, pp.57-9.

FIRST OUTDOOR SOWINGS IN SPRING

These are mainly of spinach, chards and lettuce, and also perhaps one sowing of rapid-growing mizuna which just has time to crop before the longer days make it rise to flower, and before flea beetles become too numerous. Early spinach sowings are best with varieties such as *Tarpy* (round leaves) and *Galaxy* (pointed leaves), whose growth is especially fast. They need

BEST OUTDOOR SOWING DATES
FOR OUTDOOR GROWING

MAR	APR	MAY	JUN	JUL	AUG	SEP
(from mid-month)	Lettuce	Lettuce	Lettuce	Lettuce	Lettuce (after mid-month for over-wintering only)	(All before mid-month)
Lettuce	Spinach	Spinach	Chards	Spinach		Mizuna and some other oriental leaves
Spinach	Chards	Chards	Certain varieties of endives, leaf and heart	Chards	Spinach (until mid-month)	Rocket
Chards	Peas	Orache		Any endive		Lambs lettuce
Peas, for shoots	Orache	Certain varieties of endives	Leaf chicory	Any radicchio	Chards (until mid-month)	Winter purslane
Orache	Parsley		Certain varieties of Radicchio	Sugarloaf chicory	All endives (until about 10th)	Land cress
Parsley	Coriander	Leaf chicory		Kale		
Coriander	Dill	Chicory (for forcing next winter)	Chicory for forcing	Chinese cabbage	Leaf endive (until about 20th)	
Dill	Sorrel		Kale	Rocket (better at month's end)	Leaf chicory (until about 20th)	
Sorrel		Parsley	Parsley	Oriental Leaves (better at month's end)	Kale	
		Dill	Dill	Lambs lettuce (better at month's end)	Rocket	
		Sorrel	Sorrel	Purslane	Oriental Leaves	
			Basil	Parsley	Lambs-lettuce	
			Amaranth	Dill	Turnip for leaves	
			Purslane	Sorrel	Parsley (early in month)	
				Chervil (better at month's end)	Sorrel (early in month)	
					Chervil (early in month)	
					Winter purslane	
					Land cress	

frequent picking if you want to keep eating small leaves and will crop for about a month before flowering, so make a second sowing four to six weeks after the first one.

Lettuce is much longer-lasting if you pick its leaves carefully. I thin out seedlings to about 20cm apart in rows 25cm apart (8" x 10"), which allows me to pick off outer leaves for up to three months before flowering. A second sowing of lettuce can therefore wait until about ten weeks after the first one, often in late May.

On the other hand, if you do not thin lettuce and cut across the rows of close-growing seedlings, they tend to develop more mildew on their bottom leaves and to run out of room to grow, making them flower somewhat earlier. Hence more sowings are necessary and the second one needs to be about six weeks after the first. For lettuce hearts, three-week intervals are necessary on average, but only ten days in July.

LATER OUTDOOR SOWINGS

A basic calendar of outdoor sowing is set out on the preceding page. The most tricky month is August because the frequency of sowing increases as day length diminishes rapidly, so that missing a week in August will delay cropping in autumn by up to three weeks. Missing a week in September is even more dramatic. If you want salad in the winter half of the year, it is important to be on the ball through late summer and early autumn.

Although lettuce, endives, chicories and spinach can still be sown until about mid-August, many sowings at summer's end are of the cabbage family – rocket, oriental leaves and kales – which thrive in the relative absence of flea beetles and then in damper autumn weather with shorter days.

Slow-growing lamb's lettuce is a staple throughout winter and can be sown until about mid-September. Two other possibilities are land cress for small amounts of leaves with strong flavour, and winter purslane, for unusual texture. Coriander and chervil are good winter herbs which have a long life before flowering if sown after about mid-August – but their production of winter leaves will be small unless given some shelter from the weather (see Chapter 17, pp.157-64).

Final outdoor sowings are usually sometime in the middle of September, when rocket and mizuna are probably the most likely to succeed and to continue growing slowly through any mild winter weather.

Later sowings may succeed but are dependent on the autumn being warm. Within these timelines, we can find even better sowing dates thanks to the moon.

SOWING INDOORS

THE ADVANTAGES

Using covered spaces for sowing is rather more work, but brings many benefits:

- Faster and more reliable germination enables earlier cropping in spring, when leaves are often at a premium.

- Raising plants in a separate growing space enables rapid successional cropping because you can have plants ready to set out as soon as an earlier batch of plants has reached the end of its life. This avoids periods of scarcity while waiting for seeds to germinate.

- Slugs can be avoided; it is easier to keep most plant-raising spaces clean than the whole garden.

- Pests in general are less problematic than with outdoor sowings because seedlings are growing strongly in ideal conditions and are therefore of less interest to predators.

SUITABLE SPACES

Locations for indoor sowing are varied and their use is more fully explained in Chapter 19, pp.174-90. They are listed here briefly in order of effectiveness and ease of use:

- Glass greenhouses are lovely to work in, have excellent light levels, and hold onto a little more heat at night than most plastic-coated structures.

- Polytunnels warm up well by day but lose heat rapidly at sunset. Their light levels are mostly good if the polythene is wiped annually.

- Conservatories usually have light on one side only, so growth may be less solid, but they are often warmer than outdoor structures. If it is a smart conservatory, remember that raising plants can be a slightly messy and watery business!

- Cold frames and cloches are effective at helping earlier growth but are more difficult to manage – slugs often invade and there is no room for the gardener to work in them under cover.

- Window sills are warm and cosy but can be somewhat lacking in daylight, making for leggy growth with long fragile stems, so plants must be moved to full light before they are too big. As with conservatories, watering can create mess.

MATERIALS NEEDED

- Seed trays have just enough holes in the bottom to allow excess moisture to drain out; too much water is inimical to seedlings which may then 'damp off', the term used for the often fatal attacks of mildew on baby leaves. It is best to water seed trays at the start of a bright day when sunlight will soon evaporate water from the surface of small leaves. Seedlings can be 'pricked out' into modules or pots when they have just two leaves and no more than 2-3 cm (an inch or so) of root. Gently squash the root into a pencil-sized hole in compost-filled modules, holding the seedling by its leaf, never by its tender stem.

- Module or plug trays enable the roots of each plant to grow independently, allowing rapid, undisturbed and more pest-free growth after planting. They come in various shapes and sizes, any number between 24 and 60 partitions in an A4-sized tray is good for small but sturdy plants. When filling them, press compost in firmly so that a compact and extensive root system can develop. Drainage is good in modules and damping off should be rare. Like seed trays they are usually made of plastic or polystyrene, which can be used time and again if handled gently, without any washing or cleaning. Small plugs or pots made of coir or other natural materials can be planted in their entirety but are more expensive as they serve only once.

- I recommend organic, multi-purpose potting compost if you can find it, because I believe that natural sources of nutrients are better balanced, and because their basic media are mostly recycled waste products. This may result in some weed growth, and the same is often true of sieved home-made compost. Special composts for sowing often include sharp sand or other ingredients to increase drainage.

- A good watering-can is vital and a good rose is essential, because it is important to distribute water evenly and gently, with good control so that over- and under-watering are avoided. Watering is a skill to be learned and you need to develop an awareness of the needs of your plants by watching the weather above all: plants may require as much water in two sunny days as in a dull week.

- Extra heat is only required in late winter and early spring but it is not vital. I use a bench of sand with an electric cable to warm it, set at 16°-20°C (60°-68°F). Conservatories and window sills will have enough ambient heat, so they can be good to germinate seedlings and get them underway – the first two weeks is when heat is most useful to aid in initial germination and establishment.

- Tool-wise I recommend a pencil for any pricking out and then a dibber for making holes to set plants into ground, bed or container.

A SPECIAL WORD ON USE OF MODULES

Module is a horrible word, and a fantastic way of raising plants. Each plant can develop healthy leaves and a strong root system, which survives intact when planted out. This helps to sustain it after planting, in the face of cold nights, dry days and attack by slugs. Plants can be set out at their final spacing with no need for later thinning, and where weeds are a problem you will be gaining a significant head start. Plants can be raised earlier, their growth is more predictable and less seed is used because germination is usually more even and successful.

It is highly worthwhile to spend time and money on raising good plants because they are at least half of the story.

PLANTING OUT

Use a dibber or small trowel to make small holes no larger than the root system of the plant or module/pot size, then push them in firmly, at spacings given in Part Three. Water in gently unless it is about to rain. See also the advice at the end of this chapter.

After planting them out and before picking begins there is a period called 'growing on', which is often remarkably brief for salad plants.

GROWING ON

If you have sown your seed or grown your plants in their right season, they should pass quite quickly from being tender youngsters to a stage of early maturity when the first leaves can be harvested. Salads are almost the only vegetable to make the transition so speedily – there is relatively little waiting involved, unless you want large leaves on your plate.

SLUGS

The main pest is always slugs and picking them off by torchlight is an effective way of reducing their population – on three or four successive nights if possible. You may be surprised on the first night at their numbers and level of activity. See Chapter 8, pp.60-5 for more details.

ANTS

Ants are less rapid than slugs in their depredations, but harder to control, partly because of their sheer weight of numbers. Again, see Chapter 8, p.65.

WEEDING

Two ongoing jobs are weeding and watering, both dependent on the weather. Damp weather encourages weeds to germinate and also makes it difficult to hoe, but large quantities of salad leaves grow in such small areas that weeds should rarely be a major problem. I usually pull out the few I see whilst picking leaves. I recommend you remove them while small so that they do not hide slugs under their leaves, or compete with salad plants for moisture and nutrients.

WATERING

As long as your soil is well composted, watering is only necessary in prolonged dry weather or in extreme heat. At these times, a good soak every few days is as viable as a daily sprinkle and is a more efficient use of water, because surface evaporation happens less regularly.

Should it become truly hot and sunny, say 25°C (77°F) or higher, watering every two days is worthwhile and containers will probably require water every day, as their limited volume of compost can hold less water than beds and garden soil.

It is an interesting paradox that although salad leaves are mostly water, they often grow better in fine weather because extra sunlight encourages stronger, more healthy growth; whereas in wet weather there is often too high a proportion of water to light, making leaves more sappy, softer and more vulnerable to slugs. We can add water in dry weather but we cannot add sunlight in wet weather!

FIRST HARVESTS

How to decide when your salad plants are ready to tolerate removal of a leaf or two? They need to have grown to the point where there are sufficient roots to rapidly enlarge existing small leaves and to make new ones. For well spaced lettuce, this means a plant the size of a side plate with about ten leaves altogether, of which up to four can be removed at one pick. Plant size is important as well as leaf number – rocket and spinach have fewer and larger leaves, mizuna has more, smaller ones.

If you have sown thick rows and plan to cut across the top of them, to give you a harvest of small, tender leaves, start cutting before or as soon as you see some yellowing of leaves at the bottom. This should give plenty of small leaves, and another two or three cuts, providing the knife or scissors always pass just above the top of plants' tiniest leaves.

A rule of thumb is that leaves should be picked when they start touching the leaves of neighbouring plants, for three reasons:

- They should be large enough
- Slug numbers will be prevented from increasing when soil or compost becomes covered over by leaves
- Lower leaves that are deprived of light will begin to suffer from yellowing and fungal problems

See Chapter 2, pp.16-22 for more detailed information on ways of gathering salad leaves.

FINAL FLOWERING

Picking leaves off the same plant can continue for weeks and months, until central stems begin to elongate and rise upwards, indicating that plants are finally ready to flower and set seed.

I emphasise here that if you follow my guidelines for sowing plants in their right seasons, and for regularly picking their leaves, this flowering can be postponed sufficiently to give you the most worthwhile harvest of leaves. They should be of a superb freshness and quality, with minimal damage from pests – see also Chapters 7 and 8 for more details on boosting the health of your plants, and on coping with pests.

INDOOR SOWING DATES FOR EARLIER SALAD OUTDOORS

If you wish, all the salads in the table on p.49 can also be sown indoors, while the ones listed below require extra warmth when sown in the months listed here. In an outdoor greenhouse or polytunnel, these dates work best with the provision of a little extra heat (see also Chapter 18).

JANUARY	FEBRUARY	MID-APRIL	MAY
Lettuce	Lettuce	Basil	Basil
Spinach	Spinach		Amaranth
Mizuna	Mizuna		Purslane
Parsley	Orache		
	Parsley		

PLANTING INDOOR-SOWN PLANTS

Indoor-grown plants can occasionally come ready to plant out when conditions outdoors are a little too cold and windy. Grow them as large as possible and then harden them off outside in trays or modules.

Fleece makes all the difference when planting in such conditions, protecting them from lashing winds and extremes of cold. Keep it tightly in place for up to a month – plants are happier when fleece is held firmly on top of them, than when it is loosely flapping in the wind. Just make sure to plant into clean soil and compost, with no hiding-places for slugs, which are happy under fleece and also love tender, newly arrived plants. Keep a careful eye out for them during your salads' first fortnight outside (see Chapter 8).

Chapter 7

Cosmic Leaves

Bringing new energy to soil, plants and ourselves

THE MOON

Moon forces are as mysterious to Western civilisations as is the power of water. Both are intimately related, as tidal movements remind us all the time. Salad leaves are mostly water, so the moon's behaviour is worth paying attention to.

I have grappled long and hard with understanding the best way to work with different phases of the moon. They are constantly transmitting different energies, starting with the most obvious dichotomy of waxing and waning.

Waxing/waning

Waxing moons are associated with qualities of expansion, vigour and masculinity. Waning moons are associated with qualities of contraction, passivity and femininity.

Big bold salad leaves should therefore come from sowings made in the fortnight or so of a waxing moon (see below). Those sown during a waning moon should have smaller leaves and perhaps more extensive roots. This understanding creates an approximately fortnightly rhythm and changeover points, with the whole cycle from new moon to new moon taking 29.5 days.

The zodiac

Many gardeners sow by different moon phases, created as it crosses the field of heavenly constellations which we see from Earth. During the two

or three days in front of each one, the moon picks up and transmits one of
their four different qualities: earth, air, water and fire. These translate into
encouraging one main aspect of plants' growth: roots, flowers, leaves or
fruits/seeds respectively.

For salad leaves we should look to sow seeds when the moon is in front
of one of the three water constellations – Pisces, Cancer and Scorpio. This
way of understanding moon forces involves a more rapid rhythm and "leaf
days" re-occur about every ten days.

Ascending/descending

A third change in the moon's behaviour is its height in the sky, which varies
from high to low and back again every 27.3 days, just as the sun varies
over 365 days. When living in France I noticed that many old Gascon
farmers paid more attention to this than to waxing and waning. In particular, planting out and moving plants is better during a descending moon
because root development is favoured during that fortnight.

Other periodicities

Further moon happenings serve to complicate the picture even more, such
as apogee and perigee as the moon moves closer to and further away from
Earth. Its conjunctions with and oppositions to other planets, especially
Saturn, also bring different qualities into play, as does the hour of moonrise; if you are interested, you can check out a biodynamic planting calendar or wall-chart (see *Resources*).

MOON RESEARCH

Many farmers, gardeners and scientists have run experiments where seeds
are sown at different times, principally according to waxing/waning and to
the zodiac, but also to time of moonrise. Nick Kollerstrom describes these
succinctly (see *Resources*) and they give plenty of food for thought.

Over seventy years ago there was a stunning piece of work conducted
by a Russian scientist called L. Kolisko, first published in 1936 (see
Resources). Ms Kolisko worked closely with the Anthroposophical
Agricultural Foundation in Stuttgart and grew many different plants over
a decade, sowing them at all different phases of the moon. Interestingly, she
was principally looking at waxing and waning, asking herself this simple
question:

"The forces which stream through the earth at full moon must differ
from those at new moon. Does the plant respond in its growth to these
forces or does it not?"

Kolisko's results

One major conclusion stood out above all others: growth of plants which were sown **two days before full moon** resulted in the greatest encapsulation and expression of moon forces. Plants sown then were larger and more productive of leaves, flowers, fruits and roots. Notable differences in vigour lasted to the end of their lives and were such that, for example, maize sown two days before new moon matured later and grew smaller than maize sown a fortnight or fifteen days **later,** but two days before full moon.

Two days before new and full moons is the high point of waxing and waning forces respectively, but translates to seeds only if the soil is and remains damp at that time. Water is needed to carry moon forces into Earth.

Sowings on the actual day of full moon acquaint seeds with a moon that is just beginning to ebb. Kolisko found the waning influence to build up until two days before new moon when its peak lasted a day at most, such that by the actual *day* of new moon, the force was a small waxing one.

Her book is full of photographs of many different farm and garden plants sown at different moon phases, at different stages of growth, repeated year after year in both laboratory and open ground, and all demonstrating the same result.

Implications

This carefully conducted, extensive and well documented research has a clear message: growth is strongest from sowing two days before full moon. But what if you are on holiday or otherwise occupied at that moment? How can a grower like me sow everything in one day? Or if the soil is dry, moon forces cannot enter! There is much food for thought here.

In broad terms, I aim to sow and set out salad plants in the waxing fortnight, two days before full moon when possible, as well as paying attention to the qualities associated with each constellation.

And most of all, I like to work with my green fingers, fertilising the garden with gratitude, goodwill and continual amazement at such abundant, healthy growth. Gardening at Lower Farm is a combination of the weather, my thoughts, my actions, the water I use and the moon timings I co-operate with. This is about cultivating health, as much as avoiding pest and disease.

See *Resources* for pointers to finding out more about the moon and water.

Chapter 8

The Unwanted

Coping with slugs and other pests

BRIEF SUMMARY

- *Slugs are the main pest*

- *Having clear space around the growing area is vital, to minimise accommodation for slugs*

- *Pay special attention just after sowing and just after planting anything Slugs love moisture and darkness, so keep surfaces clear of weeds, mulches and large objects, and avoid watering in the evening*

- *Be prepared, in damp weather, to foray at dusk in search of invading or emerging molluscs*

- *Have a look under larger leaves for slugs and snails sheltering, awaiting nightfall*

- *Disposal is up to you; squashing underfoot or puncturing with a pointed knife saves any handling*

- *Dry weather sees less damage but things can change fast when the weather changes*

- *Small-leaved, regularly picked salad plants are easier to keep slug-free than larger hearting specimens*

- *Slug traps, barriers and nematodes all work to a point but require regular maintenance.*

- *Sowing seasonally is important as plants are then stronger and more resistant to attack. This is especially true for avoiding most flea beetles*

- *Aphids are seldom a serious problem because they have many predators such as ladybirds*

There is no doubt about the main difficulty in growing many vegetables, and salad in particular; hungry and slimy, they slither out in the damp and the dark, heading for tender leaves, YOUR tender leaves which you recently planted. When you go out in the morning, bare stalks of once promising plants await and you have to start again, with an extra month's wait for salad.

I have known that feeling so many times, more than enough to make me ask myself *every* time I sow or plant anything at all, "is this going to grow away from slugs and snails?"

With the benefit of experience, I suffer fewer losses, and always learn some more about the behaviour patterns of slugs and other pests, when plants are eaten. In this chapter I will pass on the lessons I have learnt so that you also have more chance of watching plants grow to fruition.

THE SLUG'S ROLE IN THE GARDEN

I never knew a garden without slugs and snails, yet growth is often still bountiful and healthy. So why are they there? What role do they have?

Waste disposal is their life's work, and difficulties arise for us when their understanding of waste does not agree with ours. Mostly they are clearing up decaying vegetation in less visible areas of darkness and moisture – quite helpful, really. But sometimes if the season is unusually wet they may breed excessively and need to expand their menu. Or we may sow or plant something weak, or at the wrong time, or in a place where it will struggle. Slugs then receive the signal to go to work. . . .

TRICKY TIMES

Timing is critical. The most difficult moments are always just after sowing and planting. Slugs love baby leaves and can eat a lot of them very quickly, clearing a potentially large harvest before, say, Venus has even set in the evening.

Slugs also have a feel for plants which are not happy and thriving, especially those which have been transplanted. The act of moving a plant definitely weakens it and there is a critical period for about ten days after planting when most of its energy is needed for settling in, making it less able to resist slimy nibbling. See pp.63-4 for tips on helping plants through these difficult days.

YOUR GROWING SITE

Slugs are all moisture and slime so they mostly live undercover or in damp crevices. Any walls, piles of stone, leafy bushes and overgrown areas are slug havens, and the further from them that you can situate your salad beds or containers, the safer your leaves will be.

It will also make a difference if you can manage a slug hunt to reduce their numbers, by looking under those loose stones and large leaves, in cracks of walls near the ground, and in any damp, shady area nearby. You will soon become acquainted with their favourite spots which new arrivals will always frequent – so regular checking is worthwhile, especially in damp weather.

WEATHER

It makes all the difference if dry conditions predominate, to the point that slugs seem to almost disappear. One relaxes. But they are able to lie dormant for long periods, and then reappear rapidly when it rains so that, suddenly, they need fighting off again. Should the weather stay wet for more than a fortnight in summer, slugs thrive and breeding is rapid As numbers increase and days remain damp, one has the unusual pleasure of seeing more of them by day. Through and just after any such wet spells in the growing period, regular patrols at dawn and dusk become important and are the most effective way I know of reducing numbers.

SLUG POISONS, TRAPS AND DETERRENTS

Synthetic slug pellets, usually of metaldehyde, work by drying the slugs' slime so that they grind to a halt and then shrivel. Such pellets are highly effective *and are needed in tiny amounts*, but unfortunately the affected slugs are then poisonous to birds, pets and hedgehogs who may eat them.

Some other slug pellets, described as organic and made of ferrous phosphate, work in a similar way and claim not to leave a poisoned slug, just a dry one. But I have found they do not prevent damage to leaves in seriously sluggy conditions, and I am not entirely happy about spreading all that iron and phosphorus on my garden. There is also a gel which makes similar anti-slug claims, but again I have not been impressed.

Nematodes which invade slugs' insides are more effective, but are expensive and relatively short-lived – after watering them on soil or compost, they are effective for about six to eight weeks. It may happen that you water them on at the beginning of what turns out to be a dry spring, in which case they are a waste of time and money. They are not a complete answer by any means.

A different approach is traps, filled with attractants which collect and imprison slugs. Home-made ones such as a jar of beer at soil level are just as effective as expensive offerings in shops and catalogues. But remember that they need more or less frequent disposal of their slimy contents and then refilling, meaning less beer for the gardener.

For container-growing there are extra products, mostly based on copper and its minor electrical charge, which slugs dislike. You can buy copper-impregnated mats for pots to sit on and copper bands to attach around rims of containers. Neither will work if there are slugs or slug eggs in the container's compost already, or if a leaf grows over the top of the band and affords an entry passage to newly arriving slugs. Copper deterrents do not reduce slug numbers in your garden or patio, so they will be eating something elsewhere. Some athletic slugs have even been observed arching upwards and over the top of copper bands.

All of these so called organic remedies and means of prevention need to be taken with a pinch of salt (also good at drying slugs out), and often require more effort than simply killing a few slugs at dusk or dawn.

SLUG DISPOSAL

If you are too squeamish to kill slugs, they need removing a long way from your garden and not too close to somebody else's! I feel it is better to acknowledge that we are talking life and death here – slugs' death or your plants' death. If your plants die, no crops will grow and you may be buying supermarket vegetables which, unless they are organic, will often have been grown in relatively lifeless soils and treated with some poisons. Even if organic they will be nothing like as fresh as your produce and will not give you the same life force as fresh salad from the garden. It seems to me much healthier all round to kill excess slugs, quickly and mercifully with a firm boot or sharp knife.

GETTING PLANTS UNDERWAY SAFELY

Since most slug problems occur when seedlings are newly emerging and when plants are recently set out, you need to be extra vigilant at these times. I find April a rather nervous month, as so much new growth is just beginning, and certain other periods in the rest of the year when I have recently planted tender salads.

Aim to make your plants as tough as possible before planting out. Grow them as large as the modules/pots/seed trays and compost allow, give them three or four days of hardening off outside if they have been raised indoors, and plant them in soil or compost which has been clear of weeds and surface debris for at least a fortnight beforehand.

Sow in season

Another sure way to better growth of young plants is by **sowing plants in season**. I can't say this too often or loudly enough, because so many seed packets offer vague information, encouraging sowing too early or too late.

There are many pointers elsewhere in this book towards a balanced, seasonal approach to healthier growth. Two examples of what can happen if you sow at the wrong time will make this clearer:

Sowing too early, before soil or compost has reached a high enough temperature for fast and vigorous growth; lettuce may germinate outdoors in February, but will then almost certainly grow so slowly that one nibble by a passing slug will finish it off. Mizuna sown before July will rapidly flower and suffer many flea beetle holes.

Sowing too late, such as spinach in September; this results in weak growth and leaves full of slug holes.

Slug preferences

Once I did a trial of unseasonal salad and sowed Chinese cabbage in April. It was helped by rain in June to make a minimal heart which I harvested just as it was turning into a flowering stem. But tucked inside the outer leaves were *seven* large orange slugs, while next to it was an endive with no slug holes or slimy inhabitants. In other words, slugs have clear preferences, and if you grow healthy plants in season which are less interesting to them, you will suffer less damage.

Pak choi provides another example of this. Whenever and wherever I grow it, there are always more slug holes than on nearby plants of different species. Only a late July to early August sowing of pak choi has, in my opinion, a fifty-fifty chance of growing strongly and healthily enough to resist those almost inevitable nibbles.

A good growing medium

What you sow into makes a big difference as to whether slugs are interested or not. Out in the garden I find that well composted, undug soil has a good chance of encouraging growth that is healthy and fast enough to resist occasional slug bites.

When growing in containers, use a good organic compost so that plants grow healthily and vigorously and are able to tolerate a few nibbles. After a crop finishes, container compost can be resuscitated by incorporating, for example, some alfalfa or lucerne pellets to restore nutrient levels (see Chapter 4, p.33).

Keep harvesting, to help with weeds as well as slugs

Once your healthy, seasonal plants are growing strongly, you can look away briefly (so briefly) because they will be offering leaves to pick in as little as two to three weeks from planting time. Regular picking of small-

Lettuce in new salad bed (from front) *Bergamo*, *Bijou* and *Chartwell*

Salad rocket in a window box

Spring onions, coriander *Confetti* & chard *Ruby* – May

Radish *Rougette* – early May

Wooden frame for yard bed, on gravel

Layer of horse manure, green waste being tippe[...]

Bed filled with compost and netted against cats

First planting of lettuce – 11th March

Lettuce in terracota container (from front) *Bergamo*, *Mottistone*, *Solstice*, *Catalogna* and *Grenoble Red*

From left, lettuce, coriander flowering, peas for shoots and lettuce in yard bed – June

Bed in greenhouse for micro leaves – 56 kinds, sown 6th August

Ten days after sowing

Sixteen days after sowing

Mustard *Red Giant* – April

Pak Choi in tunnel – February

Radicchio *Lusia* after frost

to medium-sized leaves will keep slugs to a minimum – larger leaves always offer them a hiding place.

Another reason for continual small harvests is weeds – large leaves can hide weed seedlings as well, so each picking is an opportunity to remove any small weeds, which also helps to keep slug numbers down. Continual weeding of little weeds will soon clear soil of residual weed seeds so that it becomes simpler to grow nice crops.

OTHER PESTS

Apart from year-round slugs, most pests have particular seasons of prosperity and if you avoid these, your leaves will certainly be healthier. I also recommend that you accept small amounts of damage, because it is healthy for gardens to have a few pests, as this means there will be a background population of their predators.

Ants

Secretion of formic acid by ants eventually poisons roots, making leaves wilt as plants slowly die. Keeping soil moist in areas where they invade is an important deterrent, but this can be difficult along wooden edges of beds. I do not have a reliable answer here – boiling water is recommended by some, but it has not worked for me in beds where there is a huge mass of material to heat up, and I do not like its effect on worms either.

Aphids

Here is an eloquent demonstration of why insecticide should be avoided, and a demonstration of how a balance between predator and prey is always evolving, yet is often invisible to us.

When scientists are studying aphids, and their aphid colonies start to diminish, they have a way of reviving them. **They kill them all by spraying aphicide!** This works because the poison kills all insects, the pests *and* their predators, but it is the aphids which re-colonise and proliferate most quickly.

On the few occasions I notice aphids on leaves and plants, I leave them be because ladybirds usually arrive soon afterwards, whereupon the aphids diminish to insignificant levels. Only very occasionally do the aphids proliferate, for various reasons.

Severe infestations of aphids often point to plants that are unhealthy and are an indicator to the gardener that something is not quite right, for example that the soil is too dry, or the plant is growing out of season. Aphid numbers can often be reduced with water alone, as they prefer dry leaves and plants which are suffering some moisture stress.

Flea beetles

These small black, hopping insects are attracted only to brassica leaves – mustards, rocket, kale, pak choi and so forth (see Chapter 13, pp.117-128). Their main season is spring and early summer so later sowings in July and August are much less affected, and any leaves that grow in winter are especially clear of the little beetle holes.

Fleece or mesh can be used to reduce attacks by flea beetles, but it is mostly easier to sow in season and grow leaves such as lettuce and spinach in spring, which are of no interest these beetles. The odd thing is that just one out-of-season rocket plant in the middle of many lettuces will some-how be noticed by them, and its leaves will soon be full of holes, especially in dry weather. As with aphids, watering can help but only marginally in the first half of the year.

Rabbits

Many rural gardens suffer from rabbits, and some fencing or netting will keep them out. However, they are not easy to deter, and if damage is severe, growing salad in containers near the house may be your only answer.

Woodlice

Harmless little woodlice can occasionally eat baby leaves and stems, especially of true spinach. I know of no remedy, unless you are prepared to let hens loose in the garden. Spinach usually struggles for a while and then grows away from the early nibbling.

Part Two

SALAD LEAF
SEASONS OF HARVEST

Chapter 9

Leafing through the Seasons

Changing ingredients through the year

Salad leaves vary through the year. Their seasonal qualities can be separated into four overlapping yet quite different periods of harvest, which define the four salad seasons. Each one is characterised by its own spectrum of flavours and colours.

The seasonal boundaries are not precise but offer a framework to better appreciate which plants to sow, grow and pick at different times of year. They are not intended as the last word and some extra sowings from outside this definition of seasons will sometimes work, especially when the weather is not seasonal! The main transition points, moving slightly from one year to the next, are on average mid-April, mid-July, late September and early to mid-December. Winter is the longest season, requiring the most effort to grow leaves but its harvests are some of the most rewarding.

SPRING LEAVES FROM APRIL TO JULY

BRIEF SUMMARY OF SPRING LEAVES

- *There is a change to more numerous, larger and thicker leaves through these months*

- *Lettuce grows healthily and strongly in spring, with even some hearts by mid-June*

- *The other leafy staple of spring is true spinach, picked small*

- *Sumptuous flavours can be grown, notably pea shoots, sorrel and various herbs*

- *Other seasonal salad additions are flowering shoots, spring onions and asparagus*

These are mostly of mild flavour and predominantly green, with a foundation of lettuce, spinach and chard, from overwintered plants and sowings in February (indoors) to May. Less abundant and more highly flavoured additions include bean and pea shoots, sorrel of different kinds, a little endive, herbs such as dill and coriander, and orache for a colour that is markedly more vivid than even the red lettuces. Other spring vegetables such as asparagus, radish and spring onions can also liven up the salad bowl.

Spring is exciting – but it can also be a frustrating season. The poet observed optimistically "If winter comes, can spring be far behind?" This cuts both ways and when a biting north wind returns, one often reflects "If spring comes, can winter be far behind?"!

However, in spite of the two seasons overlapping frequently, two unalterable differences are a steady increase in day length and sunlight that grows brighter. Light is vital for strong, healthy growth, and as the weeks pass it is a pleasure to notice the extra size, thickness and vigour of all salad leaves, as well as the arrival of different ones from more recently sown plants.

The leaves of April

The first leaves in early April are still wintry in character, almost entirely from overwintered plants such as **lamb's lettuce, rocket** and some oriental greens such as **mibuna, chards, endives, chicories, kales** and **lettuce**. There should also be worthwhile growth of leaves on perennial roots such as **sorrel,** and herbs such as **parsley, chervil** and **coriander**. Overwintered **lettuce** such as *Grenoble Red* may show signs of hearting.

But outdoor harvests in April are normally small and the first sowings of lettuce, mizuna and spinach, even if they were made indoors in January or February, will not usually make significant growth until early May.

Early spring is actually the best time for growing salad under cover, because glass or polythene structures benefit marvellously from the extra light, often becoming warm enough by day to keep out any late frosts by night.

Although April's frosts will not kill overwintered salad plants, which have endured far colder weather already, there can be some damage to their larger and slightly more tender leaves, and new growth will be checked. A covering of fleece is often effective in bringing growth forward, except for slight damage to leaves where they are in contact with the freezing fabric.

Rapidly increasing day length encourages overwintered plants to switch from producing leaves to sending up a flower stem for production of seed. Endives are a good example: one minute they are, at last, developing a

tempting looking heart; then the next time you look this heart is trans-
forming into a more bitter stem. **Lamb's lettuce** likewise, after cropping
well in early April, quickly develops pretty and very small pale blue flowers after mid-month, which can be eaten but are not substantial.

The productive life of some salad plants can be increased by pinching
out all flowering stems and by frequent harvests. Regular picking of an
endive's outer leaves can stimulate the growth of new leaves for up to a
month. Rocket and chards will obligingly return to leaf creation when their
stems are removed, with the intriguing side-effect that new leaves are
smaller, stronger in flavour and slightly more bitter.

Some salad plants reserve the best flavour for their **flowering shoots** –
kale in particular, whose stems and flower buds are one of early spring's
most tempting offerings. Oriental leaves such as mizuna and mibuna send
up long thin stalks with yellow flowers that are both pretty and deliciously
sweet. And after mid-month comes the tastiest stem of all as the first spears
of **asparagus** push upwards – eaten raw they are crunchy, sweet and just
slightly salty as well.

All in all, April's leaves and flowers, although quite scarce, have some
of the year's most varied flavours, and can really lift one's mood after a
dark winter.

The leaves of May

May patrols the boundary between winter scarcity and summer riches,
with fluctuating temperatures which are so unpredictable. By month's end,
if not before, your first sowings of many different leaves should be offering regular meals.

A raised bed such as that in Chapter 3 (pp.23-30) can make a huge difference here because its compost will warm up more reliably than garden
soil, which risks remaining cold in a wet spring. Containers and window
boxes offer similar benefits of extra warmth.

Lettuces love the bright but not too hot conditions at this time of year,
and they will probably be the most common leaf in your salad bowl. The
wide range of lettuce varieties now available affords opportunities to bring
vibrant colours and textures to both your garden and table. Picking the
outer leaves off well spaced plants, or cutting leaves in more thickly sown
rows, brings the harvest date forward by at least a month, instead of waiting until June for the first lettuce hearts.

Spinach is another staple in May, with an especially appealing crunchiness to its first succulent leaves before they grow thinner with age. In warm
weather spinach grows rapidly and can be picked every other day to keep
its leaves small.

There is a small window of opportunity here, mainly in early May, for some useful oriental leaves, if they are sown early enough. I sow **mizuna** indoors in February and plant it out in late March, preferably under fleece, to have two or three cuts before it flowers and before too many flea beetles arrive. **Komatsuna** is another possibility, with somewhat larger leaves.

Sorrel should be abundant in May, initially from plants established the year before and then from new sowings in March. A few small leaves bring zest and bite to more watery lettuce, as do the last pickings of overwintered **chervil** and **parsley. Coriander** is more rapid to establish and March sowings can offer small bundles of powerful taste, when a few leaves are gathered off small plants.

Vibrant colour is provided by the odd plant of **orache**, while **spring onions** are growing well in May and can be one of the month's staples. Other options for livening up May salads include **chives** and **garlic chives** for tangy onion flavours and **chive flowers** for both taste and colour.

An exotic, delicious idea is to use the first **pea shoots**, whose regular picking encourages more to appear, all bringing a sweet taste of pea at a time of year when it is most welcome (see Chapter 15, pp.137-8).

The leaves of June

By June there should be no shortage of leaves and lettuce has really come into its own – this is probably its best month for rapid growth, glossy leaves and absence of mildew. **Leaf lettuce** can be gathered all month from plants sown in late winter, whose longevity is improved by picking rather than cutting. Many varieties offer a leaf per day at this time of year although dark red ones are a little slower. Some of the more vigorous ones such as *Solstice* may rise to flower before month's end.

Alternatively, by mid-June the first **lettuce hearts**, such as *Little Gem*, should be forming and they are a sweet temptation to grace any meal. Hearting cos and crisp lettuce mature a little later so a few of each sort is a way of spreading the season and avoiding gluts. Cutting lettuce hearts is not terminal to the plant as some new leaves should appear out of the remaining stump, but their growth is not usually significant, and regular sowing is the main option if you like hearts more than leaves.

March sowings of **spinach** and **chard** will probably start rising to flower in June so they are best re-sown in May. Pinching out their flowering stems will prolong picking time but the flavour of new sowings is better.

Some bitter tastes and firmer texture come from April sowings of **endives**, which can be treated like leaf lettuce and whose outer leaves can be picked on a regular basis. There is even a pale yellow endive (*Bianca Riccia da Taglio*) which I find pleasantly bright and uplifting in the garden and at mealtime (see Chapter 12, p.110).

Tall **spring onions** look nice in the garden and can be harvested all month. The green leaf of freshly pulled onions is much tastier and more appealing than that of limp shop-bought ones, and you have the choice of whether to pick them small or large.

June has strong herbal possibilities, especially **dill**, a few sprigs of which give a wonderfully clean aroma to salad. Floral options increase through the month, such as **coriander, pot marigold, borage, heartsease** and **pea flowers.**

SUMMER LEAVES FROM JULY TO SEPTEMBER

BRIEF SUMMARY OF SUMMER LEAVES

- *Salads become more and more varied through the summer*
- *Lettuce is gradually augmented with any or all of endives, chicories and oriental leaves*
- *Stronger tastes appear and many aromatic herby flavours are possible*

These are sown between late April and July, and are still mostly lettuce, but with different herbs such as **basil**. Interesting texture and flavour is offered by summery extras such as **purslane**. There can also be hearting **endives** by July, **radicchio** hearts by August and the first **oriental leaves** and **rocket** by early September. Colour variations come from **red amaranth** and basil, **red lettuce, yellow endives** and various shades of **chicory**. Strong flavours may be introduced with some bitter chicory and endive leaves, and **chard** is a reliable background addition. Summer has aspects of both spring and autumn, while two of its signature flavours are basil and purslane.

The character of leaf harvests can swing back and forth throughout the summer as growth is so rapid, some sowings lasting less long than at other times of year, and there is an increasing choice of salad plants to grow. A typical early July salad is as much spring as summer, and a September one can be quite autumnal, depending on what you sowed. The following is an outline of salad essence as it unfolds through summer.

The leaves of early July

Most **leaf lettuce** sown in late winter or early spring should crop until mid-July or so, at which point a late May sowing will be a good replacement and should crop through July and most of August. If you want **hearted lettuce**, sow a few seeds every fortnight until mid-July.

Endives become more prominent from now on, and leaf endives sown from early June can offer leaves throughout summer. **Leaf chicories** are another somewhat bitter option, or *Palla Rossa* varieties can be sown in June for hearting from late August; their heart leaves are crunchier and less bitter.

Spring sowings of **sorrel, dill, coriander** and even **parsley** will tend to start flowering through July so more sowings are needed by early summer. In hot weather, or in an indoor growing space (greenhouse, conservatory etc), the summer's top and most consistent flavour is **basil**. When regularly picked and with all flowering shoots removed, most basil will grow steadily until night temperatures drop in September or October. It really does not like cool, damp weather so a typical British summer is not ideal for growing it outdoors, unless you have a really sheltered and sunny spot. Look at Chapter 19, pp.145-8 for an idea of all the basil flavours you can grow.

For extra red colour, orache is now replaced by *Garnet Red* **amaranth**, whose dark, ruby leaves also look attractive in the garden.

The leaves of late July and early August

Through this peak of summer, leaves are tending to gain in flavour as the first **rocket** and a few **mizuna** leaves become available. With the leaves that are already growing this is a time of great and increasing salad variety and quantity, as leaves grow fast in warmth and long days.

One leaf to avoid at this time is spinach which tends to flower rather quickly if at all short of moisture. A delicious alternative, in dry summers especially, is **purslane** (not the winter purslane which should really be called claytonia). It thrives in hot sun and has fleshy, rounded, and succulent leaves which add a welcome bite to the salad bowl in hot summers but less so in wet ones when its growth is stunted.

The leaves of late August and September

These six weeks are a time of major evolution in leaf salads, which change from a mostly summer character to more and more of an autumn character as the weeks pass.

Lettuce begins to run into a few problems. With longer nights and damper days it becomes prone to mildew on leaves whose size and thickness start to decrease. Dry weather lessens the risk of mildew but can make it more vulnerable to root aphids, so it is less and less of a staple.

In its place the oriental leaves become extremely useful. Any looming gaps in salad supply can be filled with sowings of **mizuna** and **leaf radish**, probably the fastest growers, as well as various types of **mustards**, **pak choi, mibuna** and other less well-known varieties (see Chapter 13, pp.122-5). **Spinach** also reappears, although slugs may damage its leaves in wet weather.

Chicories are coming into high season with hearts of **radicchio** and **sugarloaf**. The former have utterly beautiful patterns of red and white to their heart-leaves, while the latter are much paler and thinner, of unremarkable flavour but a useful base to complement other, stronger flavours, such as the **basil** which should still be growing.

Endives also start to reveal their best qualities in late summer and should make large, attractive and slightly blanched hearts of sweeter leaves than their outer green ones. **Scarole endives**, with flat, soft and broad leaves, make especially tasty hearts which stand reasonably well, unlike the hearts of most **frizzy endives** which tend to rot soon after they are fully developed. Two or three sowings in July and into early August are necessary for a continuity of hearting endives through late summer and onwards.

A leaf which improves in quality through this period is **rocket**, partly because it has less flea beetle holes and partly because it often becomes larger and fleshier in mild, damp weather as opposed to dry heat. *Red Russian* **kale** is another attractive and tender brassica leaf for late summer.

By September's end the main season of rapid leaf production is drawing to a close, apart from a few notable exceptions described below.

AUTUMN LEAVES
FROM OCTOBER TO DECEMBER

BRIEF SUMMARY OF AUTUMN LEAVES

- *Leaves decrease in size until January*
- *Autumn can still be an abundant time for salads, much more than in winter*
- *Quantities, colours and tastes can be increased by using hearted chicories*
- *Flavours become stronger and slightly more bitter*

Leaves sown late, in July and August, are of a quite different, often stronger or more bitter flavour, and less aromatic. Lettuce loses its central role to oriental leaves, rocket, chicories and endives. Lamb's lettuce and winter purslane offer a mild and soft counterbalance, or you may prefer using land cress to increase the bite. Chards, spinach and parsley gradually diminish through autumn and have much smaller leaves by November. Many shades of green, from dark rocket to the pale, creamy sugarloaf, can be complemented by a range of pink and red chicory hearts and leaves.

Generally speaking, leaves in the winter half of the year are precious and to treasure, having extra appeal in meals which tend to become more starchy and dense. Is it their smallness and scarcity which makes them taste better, or is it some concentration of flavour as a result of slower growth? Or is it that plants with an ability to survive cold weather and low light levels are also possessed of special qualities which translate as top taste and healthy vitality in our winter salads? Grow some for yourself and see what you think. It is harder work than in spring and summer, but rewarding.

The leaves of October

All through October there is a massive slowdown of growth as light wanes and temperatures drop, especially after any early frost. Just occasionally a spell of 'Indian Summer' weather will prolong growth, but such warmth is a bonus and not to be relied upon. Even in mild autumns, it is striking how the relatively numerous new leaves are much smaller, making harvests less abundant.

As a result, it becomes useful to have some hearted plants available for creating larger bowls of salad, or for continual top-ups. Hearts of **endives**, **chicories** and **Chinese cabbage** are of top quality at this time of year and have crunchy leaves of many different flavours. They can be picked fresh or stored in a cool, damp place, their leaves peeled off as required.

Herbs become scarcer: **parsley** survives well in cooler weather but is slow-growing unless you have an indoor space for it. **Coriander** and **chervil** are also good for winter flavour. All these herbs withstand most frost but do not like continual rain and wind.

The leaves of November and December

From late November until March, it is only true winter plants which make worthwhile leaves, and then only in mild weather of temperatures around 10°C (50°F) by day and minimal frost by night: **lamb's lettuce, winter purslane, land cress, chicories, endives, salad rocket, mustards, mizuna, leaf radish** and **other oriental leaves.**

Some **parsley, chard** and **spinach** may still grow a little, while any **lettuce** leaves and **endive** hearts will probably be of poor quality, with mildew causing many leaves to rot.

Radicchios and **sugarloaves** are usually the only hearts to survive some frost and will be a joy to find, sometimes hidden under a thin layer of rotten foliage. Removal of all old chicory leaves when harvesting hearts will clear space for new growth of baby leaves out of the same root in late winter and early spring.

Hearts which have been stored, such as **Chinese cabbage**, can be defoliated as needed, but are unlikely to exist healthily beyond Christmas. **Chicories** grown for forcing need digging up before Christmas and setting to grow in a dark place, to have chicons in the New Year (see Chapter 12, pp.115-6).

WINTER LEAVES FROM DECEMBER TO APRIL

BRIEF SUMMARY OF WINTER LEAVES

- *Cold winters see little new growth*

- *In mild winters, lamb's lettuce, land cress and winter purslane grow slowly and surely*

- *Rocket, mizuna, mustards, leaf radish, leaf chicory, kale and spinach also contribute a little*

- *Outdoor leaves in winter are scarce, some indoor growing is worthwhile*

These are mostly from sowings in late August and September, are usually scarce and small, yet often have the greatest variety of taste and texture. Winter's slow-grown leaves are more solid and robust, possessing a lower proportion of water which allows them to cope with being frozen. They include lamb's lettuce, mustards, rocket, winter purslane, land cress, kales, leaf chicories, leaf endives and perhaps a few forced chicons. In mild winters there can also be some spinach and mizuna leaves. To cheer us up it is possible to enjoy a warming range of colour, including shiny green lamb's lettuce, dark red mustard and bright yellow chicons.

The leaves of January and February

These are the leanest months for outdoor picking. Even if a cloche or fleece is used to cover plants, little *significant* growth will happen; instead plants should suffer less damage from wind, frost and rain, yield just occasional leaves and then be in good shape for new growth in late winter and early spring. The most likely plants to offer new leaves at this time are **rocket, mustards, leaf radish,** and to a lesser extent **chicories, spinach** and **chard.**

The jewel in the crown of winter salads, however, is **lamb's lettuce** which can grow a surprising amount in mild spells of weather. Having said that, you would need a lot of lamb's lettuce to fill the salad bowl regularly because its leaves are quite small, and they are also fiddly to pick.

Indoor-forced **chicons** are a welcome standby, for their bright yellow colour and buttery bitter-sweet taste. Growth can be regulated by moving pots or bags of chicory roots to warmer or colder places indoors.

The leaves of March

All of the January and February leaves continue and gradually increase in size and weight as daylight returns.

Depending on the weather, some worthwhile **spinach** and **lettuce** leaves may be had towards month's end. The onion family make welcome appearances as overwintered **spring onions**, from sowings last August, start to bulk up, and **chives** may attain a harvestable size.

March can be a frustrating time because longer days put one in the mood for spring foods and outdoor leaves are often still quite scarce. It is one of the best months for growing leaves under cover, where glass or plastic will multiply the sun's new energy and enable worthwhile growth of oriental leaves, rocket, spinach, lettuce, endives, chicories, chard and some herbs; see Chapter 19, pp.174-190 for more details.

Chapter 10

Recipes for All Seasons

Leafy meals month by month

One joy of salads is that they offer such varied combinations of colour, flavour and texture, making for successful salad meals that are based on the skill of the gardener as much as of the cook.

My wife Susie and I found this chapter both challenging and stimulating, since the main way we eat salad is as seasonal mixtures of leaves, ten or more kinds in a bowl together with a simple dressing, itself changing with the seasons.

Yet salad leaves also lend themselves to creation of many more dishes, often in combination with other seasonal ingredients, and we hope you will enjoy some of the suggestions here.

SPRING RECIPES

Dressing for Spring Salads

Spring leaves, being mostly mild, green and tender, are well complemented by this variation of classic vinaigrette, which has the added flavour of nut or seed oils and is spiced up with mustard.

> *4 tablespoons olive oil*
> *1 tablespoon walnut or toasted sesame oil*
> *1 tablespoon cider, sherry or wine vinegar*
> *1 teaspoon wholegrain mustard*
> *Salt and pepper to taste*

- *Shake all ingredients together in a bottle or jar before using.*

❀ APRIL ❀

Salad of Micro Leaves

See photo in second colour section. These baby leaves were grown in two seed trays in a greenhouse and cut with a knife, three and a half weeks after being sown in late March. There was little regrowth because the stems were cut through.

> *Mizuna*
> *Komatsuna*
> *Golden Streaks*
> *Black Cabbage*
> *Garnet Red*
> *Rocket*
> *Ruby Chard (Charlotte)*
> *Tetona (equivalent to Lazio)*
> *Red Titan*
> *Yellow Chard*
> *Cress Cressida, leaf radish, green purslane*

The flavours are mild and varied – use only a little dressing to complement them.

❀ MAY ❀

Batavia Salad with Eggs, Winter Purslane and Chervil

See photo in second colour section. Occasional crisp hearts make a fine central feature to add volume and beauty. The one used here was from an overwintered lettuce and was ready in early May, while from a spring sowing it would be late June. If you can find fresh eggs from hens grazing the sweet grass of springtime, which they turn into deep orange yolks, this simple dish becomes a feast.

> *1 Batavia lettuce such as Grenoble Red*
> *1 hard-boiled egg per person*
> *1 or 2 handfuls of winter purslane flowers*
> *Small bunch of chervil*

- *Line a shallow wooden bowl with the outer leaves of the Batavia.*

- *Quarter the heart of the lettuce and arrange decoratively with the halved eggs.*

- *Scatter chopped chervil over the dish to add some herby tastes.*

- *Finish with the winter purslane flowers which make a decorative conversation piece – and have a zesty flavour.*

Spinach Egg and Potato Flan

This can be made either using filo pastry to encase it, or by simply oiling a fluted flan dish of 10" diameter. It is a great way to use any spinach which has suddenly grown too large for salad, and sometimes appears on the kitchen table in large quantities. The spinach is either overwintered Medania or March-sown Tarpy.

4 cooked potatoes (leftovers are fine)
50g / 2oz grated mature Cheddar cheese
250ml / 8fl oz milk
1 egg
Chives (garlic or normal)
500g spinach / 16oz
5 eggs (or 1 per person)
Salt, pepper

- *Cook, drain and chop the spinach.*

- *Mix with cubed potatoes, 1 egg, the Cheddar and milk.*

- *Pour into the flan dish and make hollows into which you break the eggs.*

- *Bake for 20 minutes at about 180°C / 350°F*

Lettuce Leaves with Spring Onion, Asparagus and Baby Amaranth

See photo in second colour section. In May I harvested the leaves of Mottistone, Grenoble Red, Bijou and Bergamo, which were grown in a window box to make this dish.

Leaves from four lettuce plants
4 spring onions, peeled and trimmed
4 asparagus spears, blanched for 2 minutes
A sprinkling of coloured baby leaves, in this case amaranth

- *Wash, shake dry and lay out the lettuce.*

- *Arrange the asparagus and spring onion on top, also the few tiny leaves of amaranth.*

- *Serve with some vinaigrette; also mayonnaise is delicious for dipping the asparagus and spring onion.*

❋ JUNE ❋

Somerset Spelt Risotto
with Sugar Peas and Pea Shoots

We were given a bag of organic pearled spelt from Sharpham Park in Somerset, and I based this recipe very loosely on a Sharpham recipe. It probably shouldn't be called risotto, and you can use brown rice just as well as spelt, but if you want to avoid food miles, spelt is a good choice, particularly as in our case it was growing in the field beyond our vegetable garden. I've called it Somerset risotto as many of the ingredients are local: butter, Cheddar, and cider. This is a useful recipe if your sugar snap peas have escaped your notice and the pods have become too coarse to eat. You need not waste the pods; they can be boiled up for stock or soup.

200g / 7oz pearled spelt
1 onion or 3 or 4 shallots
2 or 3 cloves of garlic
A handful of broad beans
A handful of peas (sugar snap or 'normal')
100ml / 3fl oz cider
500ml / 1 pint chicken or vegetable stock
50g / 2oz grated Cheddar

- *Soak the spelt for minimum 20 minutes in cold water.*

- *Peel and chop the onions or shallots and garlic.*

- *Melt a generous knob of butter in an oven-proof pan, add the onions and cook until softened.*

- *Drain the spelt and add to onions. Pour in a wineglass of cider, followed by the stock. Turn up the heat, and when it has come to the boil, cover and put in the oven on a low heat for about half an hour.*

- *Pod the broad beans and the coarser peas. After half an hour have a look and see how liquid the risotto is.*

- *Add some water if too dry and transfer the pan to the top of the stove.*

- *Steam the broad beans and peas briefly on the surface of the risotto, then you can take the lid off the pan and let any surplus liquid boil away.*

- *Lastly stir in a couple of handfuls of grated cheddar and remove from the stove.*

- *Serve this with vegetables of the season, such as steamed sugar snaps in their pods, and a side salad of raw pea shoots with bacon and garlic.*

Raw Pea Shoots
with Bacon and Garlic

- *Arrange your pea shoots on the side of the plate.*

- *Chop and fry a rasher of bacon with a couple of cloves of garlic and arrange on the pea shoots. The pink bacon looks pretty on the green shoots, and pea with ham is a classic combination.*

- *Serve with a drizzle of mustardy dressing.*

SUMMER RECIPES

Mayonnaise for Summer Salads

The great variety of summer flavours include many possibilities for eating vegetables raw, for which garlic mayonnaise is an ideal complement. Garlic comes ready in early July and fresh garlic is milder than winter garlic. If you want a summery vinaigrette, add a little chopped raw garlic to the spring dressing recipe.

> *5 cloves fresh garlic, peeled*
> *1 tablespoon wholegrain mustard*
> *1 level teaspoon salt*
> *2 tablespoons cider vinegar or wine vinegar*
> *1 fresh egg*
> *300-400ml / 10-13fl oz olive oil*

- *Some recipes specify ingredients at special temperatures for mayonnaise to emulsify, but I have happily made this recipe at many and varied temperatures.*

- Use a whisk or, for best results, a stick blender to emulsify the garlic, mustard, salt and vinegar together.

- Add the whole egg and whisk briefly to mix it in, then keep whisking as you slowly but surely add the oil.

- The mayonnaise should emulsify readily as oil is poured in, becoming thicker as more is added. Stop whisking as soon as all oil is incorporated.

❋ JULY ❋

Lettuce Heart (Marvel of Four Seasons in this case) with Avocado, Bacon, Garlic and Orache

A whole hearted lettuce makes a fantastic base for any dish, left intact here and splayed open from the top. Washing is more difficult than with individual leaves and needs some care; after washing hold it upside down and gently shake out the water. Butterhead lettuce have slightly waxy leaves which contribute their own oiliness to a well lubricated salad, even without any dressing.

> 1 hearted lettuce
> Orache leaves, about 20
> 1 avocado
> 3 rashers bacon
> A little oil for frying
> Garlic cloves to taste

- Slice an avocado into four quarters lengthwise; if it is ripe, the skin can simply be peeled off. Use it to weigh open the lettuce heart on top of small beds of orache leaves, which help to differentiate the green leaves and avocado.

- Fry three rashers of bacon (in this case I use back bacon), chop them and sprinkle over the avocado and lettuce.

- Garnish with some small cloves or pieces of raw garlic in the avocados – so that anybody who finds raw garlic too strong may remove them! I find the garlic is a good balance to the other oily ingredients.

Green Soup (feeds 15)

This soup is great for using up surplus leaves, and can be made with different leaves at any time of year when harvests are bountiful. It can be eaten hot or cold.

50g / 2oz butter
3 large onions
6 medium-large potatoes
Up to 500g / 16oz of salad leaves, whatever is in surplus
6 small cloves of garlic
1 litre good stock, or 4 stock cubes
500ml / 1 pint creamy milk
Salt and pepper

- *Chop onions and slowly cook in butter in ovenproof pan.*

- *Peel and slice potatoes, add to pan and season well with salt and pepper.*

- *Add the stock. Bring to boil, cover pan and put in a low oven or simmer gently for ½ hour or more.*

- *Chop garlic and leaves, add to softened potato and onion mix. No need to put back on heat or in oven.*

- *Liquidise and taste.*

- *Add milk, taste again and check consistency. Dilute if necessary.*

❀ AUGUST ❀

Blood-veined Sorrel and Bulb Fennel with Prosciutto Ham and Mayonnaise

See photo in second colour section. Blood-veined sorrel has a vigorous look and an arresting, lemony flavour, making this a most refreshing dish, whose freshness of taste is heightened by the slight aniseed nature of fennel. Broad-leaved sorrel works as well taste-wise, but looks less alluring. For variation the prosciutto can be replaced by smoked salmon.

Sorrel leaves
1 bulb fennel
40g / 2oz prosciutto or equivalent ham
1 tablespoon mayonnaise

- Arrange sorrel leaves in a rosette around a flat plate, leaving room in the middle for the chopped mixture.

- Peel away any old, outer leaves then chop a bulb fennel in small pieces.

- Cut three slices (about 40g) of prosciutto ham into tiny pieces and mix it with the fennel, together with the mayonnaise. Since the ham is salty and mayonnaise is usually well seasoned, no other ingredients are required.

Carrot, Smoked Mackerel and Pansy Flowers on a Bed of Green Leaves

See photo in second colour section. A simple recipe of beautiful colours, varied textures and a good range of flavours, using whatever leaves, carrots and flowers you have grown.

A few carrots
20 or so leaves of green lettuce, endive, chard and/or equivalent
1 smoked mackerel
Heartsease or pansy flowers

- Pick and wash any available green lettuce, endive and chard or spinach leaves. (In the photo are Appleby, a green oakleaf, Chartwell, a darker cos, Taglio leaf endive, which is quite yellow, and yellow chard.) Use the leaves to cover the bottom of a plate or bowl.

- Wash and slice lengthwise a few sweet, freshly pulled carrots, such as Purple Haze, which has a strong, earthy flavour and a striking band of dark purple around its bright orange centre.

- Lay the carrot sticks on top of the leaves, break about half to three quarters of a smoked mackerel into pieces and mound it in the centre, then garnish with any small pansy or heartsease flowers.

- The fish is oily and salty, so you may not want a dressing.

Basil Wrapped in Chicken Breasts with Purslane and Red Amaranth

See photo in second colour section. Purslane has a wonderful snap to its leaves, contrasting nicely with the soft chicken meat and the basil leaves which give this dish a strong flavour of summer. The rolls of chicken are held together here with phormium from the garden, a strong natural fibre, but otherwise garlic chives would serve as string.

Purslane, about 15 shoots
Basil leaves, of whichever variety you have most
A few red leaves such as amaranth or red basil
2 breasts of organic chicken
A little oil
New Zealand flax (not edible) or garlic chives for tying

- *Lay out a ring of washed purslane shoots around a large plate, and two or three red amaranth leaves as bases of colour for the pale chicken rolls.*

- *Fry the chicken breast very gently for about fifteen minutes so it retains its moisture and flexibility but is cooked through.*

- *When they have cooled slice them lengthwise into three strips. A sharp knife and steady hands are essential for this.*

- *Wrap each slice of chicken breast around however many basil leaves you want, and of whatever flavour. In this case I tied the rolls with thin strips of New Zealand flax (phormium).*

- *If possible leave in a cool place for a few hours, so that the basil flavour soaks into the meat.*

❈ SEPTEMBER ❈

Salmon with Lime Basil and Baby Fennel

Plenty of late summer flavour in this simple recipe, especially if you have a basil surplus, in which case the quantity of basil can happily be doubled since it becomes quite mild when cooked.

I cooked this when we had just given our bay tree a very severe pruning, and made a bonfire of the branches. When it had all been reduced to smouldering ashes I wrapped the parcel in a second sheet of foil and baked it for ten minutes in the ashes instead of the oven.

400g / 14oz salmon fillet
2 small bulbs fennel
At least 10 small sprigs lime basil
Salt and pepper

- *Place your fillet of salmon in a large sheet of foil. Then season the salmon and decorate with sprigs of lime basil.*

- *Quarter the bulbs of fennel and place around the salmon.*

- *Make a neat parcel and bake for ten minutes in a hot oven.*

Dark Red Lettuce with Cucumber, Cashew Nuts and Pumpkin Seeds

See photo in second colour section. The colours in this salad are breathtaking, and the flavours are excellent too! The nasturtium flowers add a zest of extra taste and vibrant colour, especially if you have *Empress of India* nasturtium.

> *1 large or 2 small cucumbers*
> *About 15 lettuce leaves, darkly coloured such as Rosemoor, Bijou or Redina*
> *2 or 3 tablespoons of cashew nuts, plain or roasted*
> *1 tablespoon pumpkin seeds*
> *Nasturtium flowers*
> *Salt*

- *Slice the cucumber and sprinkle with salt.*

- *An hour or so later, drain off the water which has been drawn out – the cucumber is now sweeter and more digestible.*

- *Pick and wash leaves of Bijou, Nymans, Foxley, Rosemoor or any available dark lettuce and arrange them around a medium to large plate.*

- *Lay the slices of cucumber in a circle around the outside of the plate, on top of the leaves.*

- *Make a small mound of cashew nuts in the middle, preferably whole ones, then have some fun decorating the cucumber with pumpkin seeds.*

AUTUMN RECIPES

Dressing for Autumn Salads

Since autumn's leaves have stronger and more bitter flavours, some sweetening of a dressing with balsamic vinegar, muscovado sugar or honey provides a nice balance, and milder oils work better at this time of year.

> *5 tablespoons sunflower or olive oil*
> *1 tablespoon balsamic vinegar (best quality)*
> *1-2 teaspoons muscovado sugar or clear honey*
> *1 teaspoon wholegrain mustard*
> *Salt and pepper to taste*

Shake all ingredients vigorously in a jar or bottle, making sure the sweeteners have dissolved.

❀ OCTOBER ❀

Whole Scarole Endive and Croutons

It feels extravagant to use a whole heart in one salad but the effect is so rich and the taste of the tender heart leaves is so fine, that plates keep getting refilled. There is no need for dressing here, as there is oil and salt in the bread.

> *1 whole endive*
> *4 slices of wholemeal bread, homemade if you can*
> *2 tablespoons olive oil*
> *1 sweet pepper (any colour)*
> *1 or 2 garlic cloves*

- *Cut across the base of the endive to free up its leaves, and discard the outer green ones (this is optional – you may enjoy their more bitter flavour).*

- *Wash and drain, then cut all leaves into about 2cm lengths and put in bowl.*

- *Trim crusts off the bread and cube it into about 1cm pieces.*

- *Fry in the oil for about five minutes until golden or dark brown (depending on the bread), and add to the chopped endive.*

- *Garnish with strips of sweet pepper and scatter chopped garlic over the top.*

Leaves in Early October with Flowers of Trailing Lobelia

Before the dark days set in too insistently, why not enjoy a leafy harvest festival in the last mild weather, when many summer leaves linger and those of autumn are still growing at a reasonable pace?

- *Mixed leaves, any or all of endive, chicory, oriental leaves, spinach, chard, sorrel and a little herb leaf such as chervil or flat-leaved parsley.*

- *Seasonal flowers such as lobelia, nasturtium, or heartsease.*

- *Dressing to taste.*

- *Wash and rinse leaves.*

- *Add your favourite dressing, such as the autumn one above, and toss the leaves.*

- *Sprinkle the flowers on top to complete a beautiful, lively dish.*

October Leaves with Prawns

These leaves look so especially good that, in the photo, I used only a few prawns so as not to hide their qualities. The flavours of fish and leaves complement each other well so when eating this salad we actually had a pile of about fifteen prawns in the middle of the dish.

Mustard Ruby Streaks
Tatsoi Rosette Pak Choi
Pak Choi Tai Sai
Prawns with shells on

- *Wash and rinse leaves.*

- *Decorate with prawns.*

Autumn Brassica Leaves with Herring and Ham

This composition celebrates some fine-looking and delicious leaves. It is a variation of the well-known combination of pork and cabbage, since all these leaves are of the cabbage family and go well with somewhat fatty and salty foods.

Handful of mibuna leaves
Handful of small to medium pak choi leaves
Handful of red-stemmed leaf radish leaves
1 rollmop herring
2 slices of ham
A few prawns if you wish
Some autumn dressing to taste

- *After picking the leaves carefully and rinsing them, lay on a plate in a pattern you like.*

- *Add thin slices of rollmop herring with small pieces of ham and a few prawns if you fancy them too.*

- *Sprinkle some dressing over the leaves and fish.*

WINTER RECIPES

Dressing for winter salads

Many winter leaves are strong and bitter so the autumn dressing clothes
them nicely. Then in January when Seville oranges come in season, you
could try the dressing recipe below.

❋ DECEMBER ❋

Radicchio in Hot Balsamic Vinegar

Radicchio hearts can be harvested when mature and kept in a cool place or
the fridge until needed. Their pretty leaves – whether red *Palla Rossa* or
Treviso or green *Lusia* – need only just enough time in the pan to soak up
the balsamic vinegar's sweet and sour tastes, becoming denser and more
richly flavoured in the process. They are well complemented by a scattering
on top of crisp, raw Chinese cabbage or endive leaves.

> *About 350g / 12oz of small whole radicchio leaves*
> *2 cloves garlic*
> *2 tablespoons olive oil*
> *2 tablespoons balsamic vinegar*
> *A few small leaves of Chinese cabbage or endive heart*

- *Heat the oil and vinegar, add the garlic chopped in small pieces and cook
  for about one minute.*

- *Add the radicchio leaves – but only briefly, for two minutes or less, so
  that they just collapse a little, and retain their colour. Any longer and
  they turn to brown mush – which happens quickly!*

- *Scatter the small, pale heart leaves on top for a striking contrast of
  colour and texture.*

Mustard Yorkshire Puddings

Try adding chopped mustard leaves to the batter for Yorkshire Puddings to
add a bit of heat! I serve these with a stew of chuck steak. (However,
mustard leaves do lose some of their pungency in cooking.)

❀ JANUARY/FEBRUARY ❀

Seville Orange Dressing

This goes well with a winter salad of mustard leaves, winter purslane, rocket, chicory and parsley.

1 Seville orange
Olive oil
Sugar to taste
Salt and pepper

- *Squeeze the orange and pour the juice into a measuring jug.*

- *Add 2 parts oil to 1 part juice, salt and pepper.*

- *Taste, and if too bitter add a teaspoon of muscovado sugar.*

Winter Salad with Lettuce, Winter Purslane, Apple and Cheddar

See photo in second colour section. A simple combination of superb winter flavours.

Leaves of winter purslane and lamb's lettuce, about two handfuls
1 apple, chopped – in this case I used Blenheim Orange
10 walnuts freshly shelled
50g / 2oz Cheddar cheese, cubed

- *Wash and rinse the leaves.*

- *Mix them with the apple, cheese and nuts.*

- *A dressing is optional, as there is so much oil and flavour in freshly shelled walnuts.*

The Garden's Winter Beauty in a Simple Dish

Leaves of winter purslane and lamb's lettuce, about two handfuls
1 apple, sliced – in this case I used Blenheim Orange
10 walnuts freshly shelled
50g / 2oz cheddar cheese

- *Wash and rinse the leaves.*

- *Lay them out around the plate, more could be used than this.*

- *Add the other ingredients, eat immediately or squeeze a little lemon juice over the apple to prevent it turning brown.*

❀ MARCH ❀

Red Chicory and Orange

A combination of rich flavours. The leaves are bitter, so the sweetness of the orange and balsamic vinegar counterbalances them. Their rich colour looks good with the orange and the tangy flavours of blue cheese make this a dish of many and varied tastes.

Large leaves of Treviso Svelta, loose-leaf chicory
1 orange, peeled and the segments cut up
100g / 3½oz Exmoor blue cheese (or equivalent such as Stilton) cut into cubes
Autumn vinaigrette with a little extra balsamic vinegar

- *Lay the long chicory leaves around a bowl, place the mixed orange and cheese in the centre and sprinkle dressing on top.*

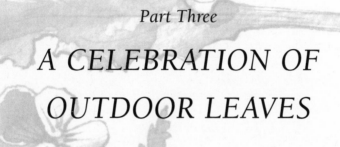

Part Three

A CELEBRATION OF
OUTDOOR LEAVES

Chapter 11

Lettuce

Clean, plentiful leaves

BRIEF SUMMARY

- *Best sown indoors January to August*
- *Best sown outdoors March to August*
- *Main season of outdoor harvest May to October*
- *Choose between picking leaves regularly or allowing hearts to form*
- *Regular picking of lettuce gives probably the highest yield of all salad leaves*
- *Young leaves survive slight frost better than mature hearts*
- *A mouth-watering range of varieties is available, with many colours, textures and tastes*
- *The main pest is slugs, but in dry summers root aphids may kill plants*

Lettuce has a lot going for it. Mild-tasting leaves of many intriguing combinations of colour, an ability to grow in relatively cool conditions and stand some frost, and the option for most varieties of producing either a heart or a steady supply of leaves over as many as three months.

The best months for lettuce are from April to July, before autumnal mildews become more prevalent. Lettuce leaves in spring and early summer have a refreshing, ultra-healthy crunchiness and glossiness, especially when grown with good compost. They are not bothered by flea beetles, so any holes are from the inevitable slugs and snails which definitely are interested in lettuce. Slug numbers can be controlled by growing leaf lettuce at wider spacings, and picking regularly, but are more difficult to control under the large, spreading leaves of lettuce hearts.

I recommend that you think of lettuce plantings in artistic terms, using them to beautify your garden or outdoor space. An appealing range of colour with different lustre and hues will then transfer, on picking, to an attractive, bountiful, and regularly filled salad bowl.

Flavour-wise, lettuce is fairly neutral: less powerful than rocket and oriental leaves, less bitter than chicories and endives, less tangy than chards and purslane. So it is fine company in salad with any of these, and especially with small amounts of stronger-tasting herbs such as basil, coriander and dill. I have fun every year, experimenting with all the additions and combinations one can make.

NORMAL PATTERN OF GROWTH

Lettuce seed germinates best in slightly warm rather than very warm soil, in spring and autumn better than in hot summer weather. Tiny seedlings grow steadily into plants up to 40cm in height and width and after three months on average, a heart of paler, crisper leaves will usually develop. This heart gradually solidifies for a week or two before suddenly breaking open and sending out a flowering stem which rises up to 90cm high, carrying tiny pale yellow flowers which eventually transform into tufts of white fluff, with clumps of pale seeds underneath them. From sowing to seed harvest takes about six months.

If a heart is not allowed to develop, through continual harvesting of lower leaves, the total harvest is often greater and always more regular from vigorous 'teenage' plants which are not allowed to mature, so that rising to flower is delayed, which then happens on a smaller stem.

Not all varieties make firm hearts and there are many different categories of lettuce, all with a range of qualities to their leaves.

SOWING AND SPACING, FOR ALL TYPES

If you sow in rows straight into a bed, I recommend a space of 25-30cm (10"-12") between the rows and then thinning plants, when they have about six leaves, to 20cm (8") apart within the row. This allows plenty of room for root development, smaller-leaf lettuce included, allowing the plants a longer life. Also some bare soil between plants makes for less slugs, especially if you pick leaves regularly (see below and also Chapter 2, pp. 16-20), and remove any weed seedlings before they develop into larger plants.

Lettuce can be sown over a long season but three sowings per year should provide leaves every day between May and October at least. Sowing

dates are mid-March, late May and mid- to late July. Also if the first sowing is under cover in January or February, for planting out in March or
early April, first leaves can be ready by mid-April, especially if plants are
covered with fleece, which is best pulled quite tight on top of them.

GROWING

Well raised lettuce plants show a sturdy resistance to cold weather. I have
had young plants out on nights of minus six degrees, frozen under fleece,
and they survived well and grew well after that. Note that hearts do not
survive being frozen, see below, p.98.

Rain is more of a problem than cold, because wet soil is slow to warm
and encourages passage of slugs at night. Snails and slugs can be a problem at any time of year, especially if it is continually wet; see Chapter 8,
pp.60-65, for ideas on dealing with them.

How your plants grow to maturity will depend on spacing, soil and
compost quality, watering and, above all, your harvesting method (see
opposite page). Weeding is the same as for other crops – do it little and
often, keeping the soil or compost weed-free for the morale of both you
and your plants.

CONTAINER GROWING

Lettuce grow well in containers, large pots and window boxes. Expect to
use about four litres of compost for each lettuce plant if you want to keep
picking leaves for at least two months. See the cropping examples in
Chapter 4, pp.34-36.

I have found that lettuce hearts are a little more tricky in containers
because slugs always seem to arrive in them sooner or later, unseen at first,
and do some deep damage. Always be vigilant for slugs especially just after
you have planted lettuce seedlings – their favourite.

WATERING

Since lettuce leaves are at least 90% water and grow quickly, their roots
need ready access to moisture. In containers and window boxes, this means
watering as often as three times a week in sunny, warm weather, or watering every three to five days in larger beds, giving the soil or compost a good
soak to at least 15cm (6") depth; this is better than a daily sprinkling which
can encourage slugs and mildew. Good compost on top of any lettuce bed
will help to hold moisture and is one reason why they thrive in it.

As plants grow larger, their needs for water increase and hearting plants

Lettuces *Bergamo* & *Chartwell* – 28th July

Same lettuce after picking outer leaves – 28th July

e lettuce on 8th August – eleven days re-growth

Same lettuce after three more pickings – 11th September, before flowering at end of Septmeber

Leaves – first picking from yard bed 18th April, lettuce and chard *Ruby*

Winter salad – Lamb's lettuce *D'Orlanda*, Winter Purslane, apples *Ellison's Orange*, Keen's Cheddar

Basil rolled in chicken breast, tied with phormium

Lettuce *Mottistone*, *Bijou* and *Bergamo* with spring onion, asparagus and baby amaranth leav

Eggs, flowering winter purslane and chervil on a bed of *Grenoble Red* lettuce

Blood-veined sorrel with bulb fennel, ham and mayonnaise

Selection of micro leaves from a seed tray,
two weeks old in May

Lettuce leaves with carrot *Purple Haze*,
smoked mackerel and heartsease

A bed of red lettuce (*Bijou* and *Nymans*) with cucumber, cashews,
sunflower seeds & nasturtium *Empress of India*

Variegated landcress – April

Chard *Ruby* – eight months after sowing

Outdoor corn salad *D'Orlanda* – April

Endive *Avance* – early April

Chicory *Treviso Tardiva* – after frost

are extremely thirsty, suffering tipburn – a rotting of the leaves' extremities – if moisture is insufficient. An advantage of regularly harvesting loose leaves is that this almost never occurs.

PROBLEMS

You will need to be constantly on your guard against slugs, the number one pest. Keeping ground clear around lettuce plants, harvesting leaves regularly and the usual slug patrols and checks are all necessary, see Chapter 8.

Root aphids are often present and then may become dramatically apparent in dry summers especially, when lettuce suddenly fall limp and then die as their roots are eaten. Consistent watering helps but some late summers can be difficult for lettuce; fortunately there are many other salad leaves to grow at that time of year.

Aphids are occasionally abundant on some leaves in early spring, again watering is a help and they usually diminish as ladybirds and other predators appear.

HARVESTING LEAVES

Picking loose leaves

I recommend picking off any larger, lower leaves by carefully holding the plant with one hand while rotating and slightly twisting one leaf at a time with the other. Always leave a central rosette of at least six or eight leaves. This is more difficult on the first pick and becomes easier as plants mature over two to three months.

At first glance it may sound more fiddly and time-consuming than either cutting hearts or cutting across thick rows of young plants. In fact I assure you that it is the other way round and that with a little practice you will find yourself quite quickly gathering a few leaves off many plants, thus composing a pretty collection, and that – barring freaky weather – they will be nearly all healthy and undamaged, as long as you remove the occasional damaged or diseased leaf at every harvest, leaving only healthy ones to grow on.

Compared with picking loose leaves, cutting a heart is time-consuming when you count all the growing time, clearing the debris, re-sowing and so forth. Careful trimming is necessary because of all the mildewed and eaten leaves which always accompany a well-formed lettuce heart.

Also I nearly always find a slug or two in my lettuce hearts, which require careful washing.

Likewise when leaves are *cut* from quite thickly sown rows of lettuce (and most other salad species), they normally need careful sorting to remove the small yellowing and diseased leaves which have been starved of light and air in the middle and at the bottom of closely growing plants. This takes time and is quite difficult to do precisely as many leaves are often just starting to go a little yellow or develop just a little mildew. Further time is lost in waiting for re-growth of the baby central leaves that have been half cut by your knife, and also from having to re-sow earlier, because cut plants live less long than carefully picked ones.

So harvest carefully and you will be rewarded! For example, in 2007 I sowed six varieties of lettuce in the greenhouse in mid-March, planted thirty-six of them out in late April on raised beds, started picking on 15 May and continued picking medium-sized leaves off these same plants, through extremely wet weather and with little slug damage, for thirteen weeks until 7 August, an average of 28g (1oz) per plant per week. Each plant yielded, on average, a total of 360g leaves.

Picking hearts

Sweetest lettuce leaves are found in their tightly folded hearts although much leaf colour is lost as leaves turn pale. Hearts develop around three months from sowing, depending on the season. Their quality is usually best from June until August, and top weights are achieved in warm, wet seasons. But if it rains and stays damp continually, many outer leaves can be lost to mildew and slugs.

A heart is mature when there is a clear definition of colour between darker outside leaves and those of a paler, tightly folded central rosette. Either slip a knife under the whole plant, and then trim off all damaged leaves until arriving at the good middle ones, or push back the unwanted outer leaves and cut higher up.

If the stump is left undisturbed, with all of its leaves removed, some re-growth of baby lettuces often occurs, but harvests are normally small.

Although lettuce plants are reasonably frost-hardy, the tightly folded leaves of hearts are damaged by freezing, mainly in October when frosts can be of sufficient duration to turn much of a heart to ice, followed by leaves rotting as they thaw.

TYPES OF LETTUCE WITH VARIETAL EXAMPLES

Batavia *Grenoble Red*

Firm, slightly crisp leaves of many colours and shiny hues. Leaves can be picked on a continual basis, leading to plants of notable longevity; otherwise, hearts of pale, crisp leaves will develop. Many varieties are winter-hardy, reflecting their origins in continental or mountainous regions of cold winters.

Butterhead *Marvel of Four Seasons*

Until recently this was the most commonly grown type in Britain, with soft, pale, waxy leaves enveloping an even paler and waxier heart. Varietal differences include a few with darker and bronze-coloured leaves, while some are winter-hardy, for hearts in the spring. The young leaves of Butterhead tend to lie low on the soil, making them hard to harvest as loose leaves, and their popularity has diminished as more people have discovered the other types of hearting lettuce.

Cos *Lobjoits*

These are lettuces of Greek origin whose growth is healthiest, for the most part, in warm summer weather. Leaves are the darkest green of any lettuce type, with some new reddish hues becoming available, and grow into sweet hearts of varying hue. Cos plants are the most upright of all lettuce and therefore lend themselves to easy picking of young leaves. A hybrid variety, *Winter Density*, will stand most winters as a small plant, then making a sweet heart in spring.

Crisp *Webb's Wonderful*

Dense, pale iceberg hearts are the usual objective when growing these lettuce. Many have been bred for commercial, evenly irrigated Californian conditions – so they heart up evenly and do best in warm summer weather with plenty of sun, yet always moist around their roots. Webbs is an older, less uniform variety with a longer season and tastier leaves, and it is rather easier to grow.

Loose-leaf *Freckles, Grenoble Red*

This category includes all lettuce which do not make firm hearts, having been bred for continual picking or cutting of young leaves. Not waiting for a heart to develop means that harvests start much earlier in the spring. The increasing popularity of leaf lettuce is drawing in an exciting range of varieties to choose from, with a wide range of colours, shapes and textures.

What is not always appreciated, however, is that many cos and Batavian lettuces are suitable for harvesting like leaf lettuce. Regular picking of their larger leaves diverts new growth from formation of hearts to growth of more outer leaves. Almost every variety of all kinds of lettuce can be picked as though it were officially a loose-leaf type. Those that best lend themselves to this kind of harvesting are recommended below.

A NOTE ON COLOUR

As well as looking strikingly different, dark red lettuce grow differently from green ones:

- they are slower-growing, sometimes at half the rate of green lettuce
- their flavour is a little bitter
- they are less appreciated by slugs than green varieties – I often notice a seeming immunity to the nibbling of nearby green lettuce. Their deep colour brings a touch of the exotic to garden plantings

VARIETIES

Most of these varieties can be treated as loose-leaf and picked regularly; if marked (H) they will also make a firm heart. Unless otherwise indicated, all are suitable for sowing from March to about mid-August.

Amorina

Amorina glows pink in almost any light, is slow to flower, but shows a slight vulnerability to mildew. Some varieties have seasons of preference and *Amorina*'s is after the longest day, from July to September. For best results, sow it from late May to June. There is a beautiful luminous quality to its deeply serrated leaves which look gorgeous when backlit by early or late sunshine. The rose-coloured leaves are fewer in number and larger than many other varieties.

Appleby

Oak-shaped leaves are pale green, compact in shape and pleasantly dense in texture. *Appleby* grows well through most of the season, from sowings between March and July. It is extremely high-yielding and long-lived, but its young leaves are a little tricky to twist off, while later pickings are easier and the payback is longevity of picking, as with *Grenoble Red*.

Bergamo

A long-lived variety, especially in autumn. Some connoisseurs are scathing about any *Lollo Biondi* or *Lollo Rosso* lettuce, because of their connection with the famous Italian film star's underwear – their frilly leaves are apparently a fair imitation of Gina Lollobrigida's pants, showy yet of little substance! However, this variety offers longevity, pretty lime green to yellow leaves and more resistance to mildew than *Lollo Rosso*. On the other hand, it is tricky to pick when young and of unremarkable flavour.

Bijou

I grow Bijou for its dark red colour alone and it grows well both early and late in the season. Like all the dark red lettuces, it looks wonderful when growing in the salad bed. It offers fewer leaves than green varieties, flowers a little earlier and has a slightly bitter flavour.

Chartwell (H)

The best cos variety I am aware of at present, with dark green leaves of compact shape, good flavour, easy to pick and reliable in any season. Also it can be allowed to grow into a heart of good flavour.

Cocarde

Vigorous growth in spring is offset by an average flavour. *Cocarde* is a high-yielding, upright oak-leaf whose rapid growth makes it worth sowing in late winter, when some other varieties might struggle a little in low temperatures, to produce heavily until early summer.

Freckles

An excellent cos variety which grows well in most conditions, and can be very high-yielding. The freckling varies from plant to plant, some leaves are covered in maroon spots and some are mostly pale green, but all leaves are thin, tender and much appreciated by slugs.

Grenoble Red (H)

A remarkable variety for consistent growth in both summer and winter, and some notable resistance to mildew and to slugs. Compact, bronzed leaves are a little tricky to pick off young plants but this is compensated for by plentiful, easier pickings as plants mature. Sow late August to early September for overwintering outdoors, it has excellent frost-resistance. Hearting can lead to tipburn if soil is allowed to dry out.

Little Gem (H)

One of the quicker-maturing varieties with first hearts by early June, from a March sowing. They are deliciously sweet and slightly waxy, but a lot of slug-eaten and diseased outer leaves usually need trimming off, especially after mid-summer when mildew invades most of its outer leaves. It can be picked as a leaf lettuce. Last sowings by late July, space closer at 20cm x 20cm (8" x 8") because the last sowings grow a little smaller in early autumn's darker days.

Lobjoits (H)

It is possible to harvest large, rather loose and pleasantly sweet hearts weighing over 1kg, especially in a wet summer, as *Lobjoits* requires plenty of water to heart up well. If too dry, the outsides of its leaves will rot, sometimes right into the heart.

Maravilla di Verano (also called Canasta) (H)

A fine summer lettuce, whose leaves are firm, shiny and mostly pale green with bronzing at the edges. It works well as a leaf lettuce or makes a characteristically pale, crisp Batavian heart. Outer and heart leaves have good flavour. Best sown from May to July as it is a little slow in cooler spring weather.

Mottistone
Quite a small cos with round, Batavian-style leaves, all beautifully mottled and bronzed. They are held close to the stem so the first few need careful picking; thereafter a steady number of leaves can be picked for up to three months as it is slow to flower.

Nymans (H)
This has pretty, quite small round leaves which are a wonderful dark red at the edge and green-red at their base. Yields are not high – it is a small cos, and it can be allowed to heart up. In catalogues I have seen it described as "resistant to mildew" but in my experience it is one of the first to suffer in wet weather.

Rosemoor (H)
Red leaves of a deep hue are quite long and easy to pick, of fair flavour and grow vigorously. *Rosemoor* crops for a longer season than many other red varieties and looks great in both garden and salads.

OTHER LOOSE-LEAF VARIETIES

Aruba
Dark red, long and rather thin oak leaves.

Catalogna
Vigorous, bright green and long leaves of unremarkable flavour.

Lollo Rosso
Slow-growing, prone to mildew, pretty leaves.

New Red Fire
High-yielding frilly, bronzed leaves, average flavour.

Rubens Red (H)
A hearting cos with tasty bronze leaves, good for picking as leaves.

Salad Bowl (Red and Green)
Thin, fragile oak leaves, prone to mildew.

Solstice
Large, frilled, bright green leaves, fast-growing and good for spring harvests.

OTHER HEARTING VARIETIES

Sow from March to July and space at 25cm x 25cm (10" x 10") unless otherwise mentioned.

Butterhead

Buttercrunch
Fast-maturing, extra waxy, pale hearts.

Marvel of Four Seasons
Sow from March to September, hardy and with an attractive rosy edge to its leaves.

May Queen
Old-fashioned overwintering lettuce, sow early September to heart in May.

Crisp

Ice Queen
On the small side with shiny, remarkably pointed and crunchy leaves.

Saladin
Standard iceberg, sow April to June, space at 30cm x 30cm (12" x 12").

Webb's Wonderful
Easier to grow than *Saladin* with a smaller, tastier and more textured heart.

LETTUCE MIXTURES

Most seed companies offer packets of mixed lettuce seed, a simple way to grow a variety of leaves. You are slightly at their mercy in terms of the mix of ingredients, which may not contain your favourites, and the differing patterns of growth may make harvesting a little more tricky, especially from a thickly sown row for cutting.

Because lettuce seed keeps so well, for up to five years, it may be more fun and practical to create your own mix of a few favoured varieties.

Chapter 12

Endives and Chicories

A remarkable range of beautiful leaves

BRIEF SUMMARY

- *Strong-flavoured leaves are firm-textured and slightly bitter*

- *Hearts are of sweeter flavour and often quite large*

- *Sow from May to mid-August for loose leaves*

- *Plants for hearting are best sown after the longest day, from June 21 until late July for chicories, and until early August for endives*

- *These salad plants are ideal second crops, to follow early vegetables such as broad beans, peas and even onions*

- *Endives have either long leaves with curly leaflets (frizzy) or smooth, broader leaves (scarole). Both have the potential to make hearts*

- *Chicory leaves have an enormous range of shapes and colours, many can be picked as loose leaves. The main hearting types are pale green sugarloaf and vivid red and white radicchios*

- *Plants survive frost better than lettuce but hearting plants are vulnerable to moderate frost*

- *In mild winters, some plants from early autumn sowing can survive and make hearts in April*

- *Slugs can damage leaves, especially of young plants. Rabbits love baby endives*

These leaves, descended from blue flowering wild chicory, deserve to be grown more than they are, in Britain at least. Their trademarks are a wide range of colours and flavours, often intriguingly bitter-sweet, and an ability to thrive in the dark days of late autumn and winter.

While being members, like lettuce, of the *Compositae* plant family, endives and chicories are different in two important ways. Firstly, as well as being more bitter, their leaves are higher in dry matter, so they offer plenty to chew on, and keep well after picking. Secondly, they need sowing rather later because the lengthening days of spring encourage them to flower, while the shortening days of autumn lead to plenty of leafy growth and also to substantial hearts when they have been sown from mid-June until early August. These are useful assets when balanced against the relatively lower quality growth and more watery flavour of lettuce in late season.

Growing these exciting hearts is not difficult when you know how to do it. By growing hearts as well as leaves, you can enjoy great contrasts of flavour and colour. Northern Italians like to eat them hot, looking on them as we do cabbages. Their more bitter flavour takes some getting used to, but they are less prone to pests than cabbage and make a beautiful feature in the autumn garden.

A further possibility is to grow special varieties of chicory for forcing. Their roots are dug up in autumn and brought indoors to a dark, warmer place for the sprouting of pale, bitter-sweet chicons.

NORMAL PATTERN OF GROWTH

Early growth is perhaps a little slower than lettuce as leaves are slightly tougher and contain proportionately less water. From sowings in spring, plants will remain rather small before flowering, depending on the variety. For example, any chicory hearts which do form in early summer, although sometimes looking promising for a while, will often suddenly break open and transform into a flower stem.

Late summer and early autumn growth is more predictable and hearts can become quite large – up to two kilograms for sugarloaf chicory. This is a great help in mitigating the leaves' bitterness and introduces some pleasantly sweet flavours.

Hearts of endives remain half open, less dense than lettuce but with proportionately more small leaves which are pale and attractive. In the damp, cooler weather of autumn they often start to rot at the edges soon after maturing; frizzy endives in particular need eating as soon as their hearts mature.

Chicory hearts last better and can also be cut and stored indoors. Once tightly folded they are at some risk, depending on variety, from the same browning at the edges as endives and this is less visible. Decaying leaves can be peeled away and sometimes a fine small heart may be found inside an outer sheath of brown, rotten leaves.

SOWING

Since most early growth is happening in warmer, drier months of the year, seedlings should be easier to bring on than those of early lettuce. I still recommend use of indoor facilities if you have them, partly because slugs are more than partial to baby leaves and small plants of endive and chicory.

As with lettuce, seed can be sown from March to mid-August, but unlike lettuce it is best to wait until close to or after the solstice in late June. A few varieties for leaves, such as *Bianca Riccia da Taglio* endive and *Treviso Svelta* chicory, are suitable for sowing as early as late April but will grow larger and for longer if sown after mid-May or into early June.

Some hearting endives will make a head in August from sowings in late May, check the varieties section below to see which ones are best for this. Otherwise, June 21 is kick-off date for best quality hearts and any sowings through July, even into early August, should have time to make a reasonable cluster of blanched leaves. In mild autumns, hearts can be enjoyed through November from sowings made in early August.

For chicory hearts, early to mid-July is the best time as sowings in the last third of July can sometimes run out of growing time before hearts of any size can develop. So there is quite a small window of sowing opportunity there, although an unexpectedly mild autumn sometimes brings late sowings to full maturity.

SPACING

Spacing for production of loose leaves is similar to lettuce – about 25cm x 25cm (10" x 10") for individual plants; this will give regular pickings of larger leaves and plants which should live longer. Try closer spacings as little as 2cm apart in rows 20cm apart (1" x 8") if you want to keep cutting small leaves.

Sowings of suitable varieties of endive in late June and July have sufficient time, in well composted and moist soil, to make large hearts, so a spacing of 30cm x 30cm (12" x 12") is the minimum if you want them to keep growing. After mid-September and into October their hearts grow paler and denser, potentially heavy and a great treat for early autumn meals.

Most chicories for hearting are potentially large plants and long-lived, so a spacing of 30cm x 30cm (12" x 12") is advisable, perhaps a little more for the sugarloaves and a little less for the Grumolos.

GROWING

Once plants are established, growth is often rapid, especially in their main season of late summer warmth. Watering will be necessary in dry weather.

As endives and chicories become large and established, they tolerate some nibbling by slugs of their older, outer leaves which often afford moist shelter to slugs and snails. At this stage it is worthwhile having a look underneath and picking any molluscs you find off the undersides of the leaves to stop them grazing on small plants nearby.

Regularly picked, leaf chicory from an early June sowing should last the whole season and even into the following spring. Earlier sowings may rise to flower in late summer.

Spacing can be in a row 30cm (12") from other plants, with chicories at 5-7cm apart (2"-3"), which gives space for them to grow healthy leaves and even some mini-hearts if you leave them alone.

CONTAINER GROWING

Leaf endive and chicory are more worthwhile in containers than hearts, which tend to fill up with slugs and become difficult to water adequately when nearing maturity; this is because they need so much water and their large leaves tend to deflect it.

Plant any varieties recommended for leaf production (see below) and harvest some every few days to lessen slug problems, make watering easier and give you regular harvests. As for lettuce, about four litres of compost per plant should provide the resources to keep them cropping.

WATERING

These fast-growing autumn salads may run short of water at a time when soil is often dry, especially when they are following an earlier vegetable crop. So moisten well at planting time and, unless it is a wet season, be generous once plants are growing vigorously from late August through September.

PROBLEMS

Slugs are fond of tender young seedlings and plants but later growth seems of less interest to them, so hearts are often mostly clean. Success is most likely from raising strong plants in plugs or modules, rather than sowing direct. Also this gives more time for preceding vegetables or salad crops to finish, as all chicories and endives make an excellent second crop of vegetables.

Rabbits seem to like endives more than any other salad, and they are not easy to fence out (see p.66).

Both endive and radicchio hearts are prone to rot at their leaf margins once fully mature; some experience is needed to learn the best moments for harvesting. Although frost may damage hearts, I find they mostly survive down to about -4°C (23°F) and colder if hearts are still loose, especially *Lusia*. If a -5°C (25°F) or harder frost is forecast, I recommend harvesting all firm hearts, then keeping them in a polythene bag until they are required, at about 5°C (40°F) if possible, and they should keep for a month or more.

REMOVING OLD ROOTS

By May, any remaining chicory roots will be starting to flower. I cut around them with a trowel and pull out the central rootball, including its largest feeder roots, then spread some compost and plant beans or courgettes or sow beetroot etc.

HARVESTING LEAVES

Loose leaves

It is not always easy to pick individual endive leaves because they tend to cluster together, lying quite close to the soil. But a pretty yellow variety called *Bianca Riccia da Taglio* has a more open habit of growth and longer, more accessible leaves, as does the green *Romanesca da Taglio*.

Some endives lend themselves to careful cutting just above their crown, about 2-3cm (1") above the soil surface. I have found *Frenzy* and *Louviers* best, offering several harvests off the same root, starting in early summer.

The most straightforward chicory is a Treviso called *Svelta*, with long, matt, oval-shaped leaves, green with red spots, turning dark red in colder weather. Plants can be cut frequently, with just a few leaves, or left longer to make a loose heart.

Hearts

Hearts vary – check the varietal descriptions to see what you should expect. Endive hearts are loose and open, chicory hearts are mostly tightly folded.

Because they are all somewhat different and do not always stand well before starting to rot – depending on the weather and exact time of year – they may not always be at their peak just when you want them but should be close to matching your requirements as long as you respect the sowing dates.

Some slug-eaten, rotting, yellowing and somewhat bitter outer leaves will need discarding when plants are cut, but there should also be a large number of pristine, beautiful, tender, brightly coloured and sweeter leaves in the plants' centres.

TYPES OF ENDIVE WITH VARIETAL EXAMPLES

Hearting Frizzy (*frisée*) *Frenzy*

Frizzy or frisée describes any endives with deeply serrated leaves. Leaves are mostly long and thin with either flat or curly 'teeth' along their length. Leaf colour ranges from dark green to pale yellow. Best season for hearting is September and October if it is not too cold; any plants maturing after that will be smaller and at risk of rotting from damp or in the event of significant frost.

Hearting Scarole *Bubikopf*

Scarole broad-leaved endives are usually grown for hearting; often of a rather pale green colour they have much rounder and fleshier leaves than frizzy endives. Their hearts can mature to a considerable size in September and are less fragile than those of frizzy endives, but you still need to watch carefully for the leaves turning brown.

Leaf Endive *Bianca Riccia da Taglio*

Some endives can be regularly picked or cut and keep producing leaves over a long period. This works well from sowings as early as May.

VARIETIES OF LEAF AND HEARTING ENDIVES

Varieties mentioned here are ones I have grown, but there are many more and I urge you to experiment with others you may come across, on foreign holidays or as they become available here. British seed companies are beginning to offer a sample of the wide range available in mainland Europe.

Bubikopf is my reference variety here and carries a detailed description which is mostly applicable to the other varieties, except for the differences I mention. The ability to make a blanched heart is marked (H).

Avance (H)

A hearting or leaf scarole. The main difference from *Bubikopf* is a slightly greater frost-hardiness.

Bianca Riccia da Taglio

Leaf frizzy. I like this variety for its luminous pale yellow colour, the relative ease of picking its long-stemmed leaves and their mild flavour. First sowings in April will crop for a month or so before flowering and add variety to the predominantly lettuce salads of spring. Sowings from May to July will crop for longer and with higher yields. Usually I twist off the larger leaves around its base but cutting is also possible, about 2-3cm (1") above the crown, and harvestable re-growth happens within two to three weeks. For this to happen, make sure the knife slices through leaves above the firm stem so that, from one horizontal cut, they will all separate without needing a further cut to part them. Leaves have attractive pink colouration on their lower stem.

Bordeaux cornet (H)

Hearting scarole. Similar to *Bubikopf* below, except that its heart leaves are longer and more pointed and sometimes cluster into a cone of yellow leaves.

Bubikopf (H)

Hearting scarole. Although the translation of this German name means baby-head, it often grows to a large plant with a well-filled, reasonably blanched heart. Best sowing dates are throughout July for maturity after mid-September, when mild temperatures and a balance of sun and rain are just what endives like. But cold nights and extreme wet can cause rotting so keep an eye on them, especially leaf margins which are the first to show faint brownness, which can quickly lead to many leaves rotting.

Young plants are more frost-hardy than hearted ones, so a late September sowing may survive until the following spring and make a small heart before flowering. Watch it closely because the flowering stem in April can quickly rob a decent heart of its best leaves. Alternatively, a few outer leaves at a time can be picked off through late winter and early spring, to provide a continual supply of smaller, rather more bitter but healthily green leaves.

Fine de Louvier

Leaf or heart, frizzy. While its growth habit is similar to *Frenzy* (see above), the leaves of *Louvier* are darker green, less numerous and a little more substantial, with thicker stems. This variety is recommended for late spring harvests but I find it works through to early autumn, although *Frenzy* is more consistent.

Frenzy (H)

Leaf or hearting frizzy. A heart of pale and finely desiccated leaves can be obtained if *Frenzy* is allowed to grow for eight to ten weeks after sowings made from June to mid-August.

Alternatively, from a sowing in May, leaves can be harvested many times off the same root between late June and September. As plants of *Frenzy* mature, their leaves become thinner and more numerous, and cutting them every fortnight or three weeks gives a plentiful supply. Use a sharp knife, horizontally, about 1-2cm (½"-1") above the plant's base. A few yellowing outer leaves will need discarding, especially after longer intervals between harvests. If spaced at 30cm x 30cm (12" x 12") the roots have plenty of nutrients and water to tap into, resulting in steady growth over a long period until at least mid-October, depending on the weather.

Glory (H)
Hearting frizzy. Larger- and darker-leaved than *Frenzy* – longer, heavier, more glossy and with substantial curly edges. Sow after about mid-June for well filled hearts; last sowings by early August will mature in October and November, when there is some risk of rotting and of frost damage to the more tender hearting leaves. A covering of fleece can save the day if it is unusually cold.

Riccia Romanesca da Taglio (also called Romanesco)
Leaf frizzy. More bitter than all of the above with large, dark green leaves which hang loose and never cluster. Regular picking works best, before any yellowing of older leaves. They grow well in cool weather but dislike moderate frost. Plants may survive the winter to re-grow for a while in early spring. New sowings in spring tend to flower before many leaves are produced.

Verde a Cuore Pieno (H)
Leaf and hearting scarole, similar growth habit to Bubikopf.

TYPES OF CHICORY WITH VARIETAL EXAMPLES

Sugarloaf Hearts *Bianca di Milano*
Large, usually tall and thin, pale green plants with folded leaves which tighten up from about September onwards. Hearts have pale, creamy-coloured leaves, thin and papery at the edge, more crunchy towards the centre. They stand frost down to about -3°C (27°F) or -4°C (25°F), but if lower temperatures are forecast, it is better to cut hearts that are mature and store in a cool place for up to six weeks.

Radicchio Hearts *Palla Rossa*
Some of the most beautiful salad leaves occur in radicchio hearts; crisp and firm leaves which are mottled or streaked in various combinations of red, white and pale green. *Palla Rossa* plants have round, red hearts of more or less tightly wrapped leaves and are usually named after their place of ori-

gin in Italy, such as Lusia or Verona. The standard *Palla Rossa* variety comes from Chioggia and is little esteemed, flavour- and texture-wise, by Italian cooks. *Treviso* radicchios have longer, thinner, more succulent and sometimes waxy leaves of intense colour. They grow more slowly, so are correspondingly highly priced and sought after. Their hearts are really a collection of smaller leaves without any tight binding – but see 'Forcing' below.

Leaf Chicory *Treviso Svelta*

Many varieties are suitable for picking or cutting at regular intervals. Chicory re-grows better after cutting than most endive and lettuce, but harvesting loose leaves rather than hearts means that they are more bitter. Leaves come in various shades of red and green and have many different shapes.

Forcing Chicories *Witloof*

Varieties of chicory bred for forcing make large roots which are best trimmed of all leaves and dug up between November and Christmas; they then need keeping in total darkness so that they grow chicons of yellow leaves. Any light will cause these chicons to open a little and become slightly bitter and green, instead of sweet and yellow. See below for information on varieties to use, how to grow the chicons and the best temperatures for bringing them on.

VARIETIES OF HEARTING CHICORY

Bianca di Milano

A compact sugarloaf. Sowing date is important if you want well blanched leaves in a firm, heavy heart, papery at its edge and crisp in the middle; aim for the week between June 28th and July 5th. Later sowings until about July 15th grow well but fold into smaller, looser hearts. These, however, will stand frost better than the large, tight ones which also risk rotting at their edges, although these leaves can be peeled off to reveal a dense, white heart. Plants with loose hearts can stand through winter for harvesting as late as March.

Grumolo Verde

Small green heart or leaf. This variety is best suited to sowing in late July or early August for standing the winter as fair-sized but loose-leaved plants, to make small and thoroughly welcome hearts in March and April. There can also be some tasty re-growth after cutting this heart. *Grumolo Rosso* grows a little smaller and with attractive red colouration. *Grumolo Bionda* is less frost-hardy and seems more inclined to heart up before winter if leaves are not picked.

Indigo F1
A new variety of red radicchio, of *Palla Rossa* type but making more uniform and denser hearts, all maturing at about the same time. This may not be good if you have only a few plants and want them to mature over a month or more.

Palla Rossa
Red radicchio (usually of *Chioggia* but not attributed). This standard red radicchio can be sown from early June to late July to make hearts from about mid-August to November, and to the year's end if frost holds off. Plants mature at different rates from one sowing and have slightly looser, less regular heads than F1 varieties.

Palla Rossa Agena
Pink and red radicchio. Beautiful variations of colour mark out this variety. Mostly green outer leaves enfold hearts of white and pink, usually in October and November from sowings in early to mid-July.

Palla Rossa di Verona
Exemplifies the difficulties I have had in finding out how to grow hearting radicchios. I have not had much luck in growing *Verona* for hearts, achieving small and loose but beautifully coloured heads. The gorgeous heads photographed on the seed packet I used look a little like forced ones and this variety should respond to being dug up like *Treviso* (see below under 'Forcing').

Palla Rossa Marzatica
Similar to Agena and a little more frost-hardy, one of the best varieties for late red hearts. Sow late July for Christmas radicchio.

Rossa di Treviso
Makes small clusters of pointed, dark red leaves in open ground in late autumn, turning almost black in frosty weather. They are striking and tasty. For extra value, try digging up the roots and forcing some small chicons, usually one per root (see 'Forcing' on pp.115-6).

Sugarloaf, Pan di Zucchero
Tall sugarloaf. Similar to *Milano* above but longer and heavier with slightly thinner leaves. It can weigh up to 2kg when all goes well.

Variegata di Castelfranco
This is an enigma, offering a loose head in late autumn of prettily speckled leaves that mostly resist frost and sometimes transform into a small heart in late winter or early spring, although I find that some plants' leaves just rot around their edges. *Castelfranco*'s roots can also be dug before Christmas to force, see below.

Variegata di Lusia
Pale pink and green radicchio. The best radicchio I know for late harvests
up to and even beyond Christmas, unless severe frost arrives early. Sow in
mid-July to very early August and watch the rather ordinary-looking pale
green plants turn into medium-sized hearts in November and December,
with some attractive maroon speckles and streaks on outer leaves and
warm pink colours inside them.

VARIETAL EXAMPLES OF LEAF CHICORY

Catalogna Gigante da Chioggia
A most vigorous plant with welcome larger leaves when many plants are
growing less strongly. Its thick pale stems can be surprisingly sweet when
a little blanched by other stems outside them and the long, fleshy, serrated
leaves are of agreeable flavour, although a little prone to browning at their
edges.

Red-ribbed Dandelion
This is really a leaf chicory and should be treated as such; best sown from
May until mid-August. Leaves are best picked or cut at least weekly, unless
you like them really long and with thick stems. Clean old leaves away in
December and look for new ones in March and April; if left beyond that,
there will grow a long and straggly stem with pretty pale blue flowers.

Selvatica da Campo
More ground-hugging than *Catalogna* with medium green, indented leaves
that are quite long and leafy to their base.

Treviso Svelta
An excellent variety for many harvests of prettily coloured leaves, more
green in summer and red in cold weather. It can be picked or cut in many
ways – remove small leaves as you need them or allow plants to grow
about 25cm (10") high with small pink leaves at their semi-hearting centres. Any unpicked larger leaves die back in late autumn but roots should
survive and make new leaves in early spring before flowering in May.

Zuccherina di Trieste
If they are true to their name, these thin, smooth and oval-shaped leaves of
pale green colour should be sweet and sugary. However, to me they taste
of normal chicory, slightly bitter and agreeably tender.

GROWING CHICORIES FOR FORCING

To grow chicons you first of all need to grow chicories through the summer and autumn. Sometimes these offer a small tasty heart but most of their leaves are large and bitter, and are trimmed off when the chicory roots are dug out. These roots are then brought indoors where, in darkness and some warmth, they grow numbers of chicons of variable size and from two to twelve or so off each root.

SOWING

Sow any time between early May and mid-June, depending how large you want the roots to grow. Slugs love the baby leaves of seedlings, so I sow two seeds per module in the greenhouse, then thin to one and plant at about 30cm x 30cm (12" x 12") in late June or early July, often after early beans or potatoes.

GROWING

Once established these chicories are robust and vigorous until November when their outer leaves start to die back, leaving a cluster of semi-hearted leaves which can be eaten although they tend to rot quite quickly.

HARVESTING ROOTS

Roots are ready to harvest from this point and want digging out carefully as any branch roots that are left behind will grow like weeds the following year. Trim off all leaves, right down to the white tops of the roots.

GROWING CHICONS

Location and temperature are important; choose from these two options when growing chicons:

1) Place in buckets or large pots so that the top 3cm (1") of roots is above the level of compost packed around the lower part of the roots. Roots can be packed in together, say three to a 25cm (10") pot, depending how large they have grown. They are best grown in a dark cupboard or shed to keep chicons firm.

2) Place two or three roots in a polythene sack or bin-liner to conserve moisture and exclude light. Roots can be laid out horizontally; chicons will grow upwards and at right angles to them.

The first method gives roots a longer life with second and perhaps third re-growths, but these later pickings are sometimes of lower quality, so the simpler second option is worthwhile and can produce some fine chicons. Nearly all of the main first crop of chicons is coming out of the root, rather than being fed from compost in a pot.

Chicons are almost the only salad whose speed of growth is controlled by the gardener. Place roots in a warm airing cupboard and chicons will appear quickly, growing to full size in two to four weeks. Alternatively, keep them at 'cellar temperature' of about 11°C (52°F) for harvests after eight to twelve weeks.

HARVESTING CHICONS

Chicons show maturity by losing a little quality on their outer leaves and then by elongating as a flowering stalk is initiated. Cut any that are like that and also thin out small chicons where a lot have appeared. Harvesting period depends on temperature: fast growth may result in one large harvest, slow growth in several smaller ones.

Final harvests are in late April to early May and roots can then be composted.

VARIETAL EXAMPLES OF FORCING CHICONS

Palla Rossa di Treviso
In their region of origin they are dug out from early November, pruned of all leaves and straggly roots, then placed in troughs of top-quality water of a mild temperature in large barns or hangars. Within three weeks or so they have grown beautiful clusters of pink, top-flavoured leaves which look like flowers and are of exquisite flavour. We cannot replicate this in the UK, but reasonable and pretty chicons will grow from roots placed in compost or bags and kept dark, preferably at a temperature of 12°-18°C (54°-65°F).

Witloof
The standard variety which I have found reliable.

Yellora
Similar to Witloof, a little more yellow colour in the chicons.

Zoom F1
Similar to Yellora, extra vigour makes it suitable for growing without compost.

Chapter 13

Leaves of the Cabbage Family

Oriental leaves, kales, rockets and others

BRIEF SUMMARY

- *Main period of sowing is late June to early September; best results often come from sowings in August*

- *Check the varied dates for each different type of plant. It is important to respect these dates for best results*

- *Most of the pests which love brassicas are less numerous after late summer*

- *Main period of outdoor harvest is mid-August to November*

- *Light frost is tolerated and a few of these plants survive extreme winters*

- *Without protection, leaf harvests from December to early March are usually small*

- *Apart from Chinese cabbage, all plants make leaves not hearts*

- *There is a huge variety of leaf flavours, sizes and colours*

- *Growth is rapid so watering is necessary, especially if late summer and early autumn are dry*

- *These are ideal second crops in the garden after peas, beans, carrots, lettuce etc.*

From the number of times I am asked questions such as "Why does my rocket have so many holes in its leaves?" and "Why has my mizuna all flowered so quickly?" I realise that the cultivation of these vegetables is rather misunderstood.

Most importantly, they are programmed to set seed when days are lengthening up to midsummer. Therefore, avoid sowing them in spring if you want leaves rather than flowers. Also, all members of the cabbage family are highly attractive to many kinds of pest, especially in spring and summer.

Look carefully at the summary below for advice on succeeding with these demanding but also potentially rewarding plants. Their virtues include rapid growth from sowings in late summer, a greater ability to survive light frosts and make new leaves in winter than most other salads, and a wide range of spicy flavours and leaf shapes, often with attractive colours as well.

Should you have an indoor growing space, their cool season capabilities can be exploited more fully to enjoy significant winter harvests (see Chapter 19, pp.174-190 for more detailed explanation).

NORMAL PATTERN OF GROWTH

Most of the cabbage family germinate in warm soil to make their main growth in the second half of the year. Having originated in oceanic, temperate climates they tolerate normal winter conditions in countries such as Britain, Ireland and Japan, as well as the coastal regions of north-west Europe, but struggle in dry weather and severe continental frost. Brassicas thrive in mild rain and moisture, as, unfortunately, do slugs and some aphids.

During winter there is little new growth but before flowering in late winter and early spring there is a short period when leaves grow and renew, especially if it has been a mild winter. This is a source of valuable salads in March and April, at a time when many gardens are bare of fresh green vegetables to harvest.

Then as days lengthen in spring they begin to develop a flower stem, often long, thin and edible when young, with bright yellow and tasty flowers which open remarkably fast in any spring warmth. Some brassicas, such as cauliflowers and broccoli, have been bred to grow larger flower buds which we eat before they open out.

SOWING

Seed of most brassicas germinates reassuringly fast, so the first green shoots are often visible within four days in summer – which is their main sowing season – from about early July to mid-September. July sowings are more likely to encounter flea beetles, September sowings may suffer slug damage as they grow more slowly.

Different speeds of growth and leaf qualities make for different best sowing dates – see the descriptions below.

All of these plants can be raised in modules or small pots, or sown direct. You will find most success with sowing under cover, especially in July when flea beetles are more numerous and can severely weaken a patch of young seedlings. Sowing indoors is best at any time for avoiding slugs. All plants in this chapter grow well as clumps, so you can sow five or six seeds per module.

SPACING

For direct sowing use row widths of 30cm (12") and thin plants to 2-8cm (1-3"), depending on whether you want baby or medium-sized leaves.

GROWING

Plant multi-sown modules at about 22cm x 22cm (9" x 9") to grow attractive clumps of leaves.

Rapid growth means high demands for moisture and in all except the wettest summers some watering will improve the quality of growth. Autumn is often easier in this respect, offering warmth and moisture in just the right amounts.

Composted soil holds moisture well, and the beds featured in Chapter 3 are eminently suitable for brassica leaves, as are window boxes or pots filled with nutritious compost and watered regularly.

Growth will slow in October, and thereafter new leaves become rather precious until new growth in March, depending on weather conditions. A cloche covering through winter will usually double the harvest at least, and a cover of fleece will increase it, though less effectively.

CONTAINER GROWING

All of these plants, grown for frequent picking, are ideal to grow in containers, particularly since they slot into a 'container rotation' as second crops. You could, for example, grow lettuce from April to July, then mustards and kale from August, or spinach from April followed by lettuce from June followed by rocket and mizuna from September. This book is full of information which can be assembled along these lines, enabling you to grow the leaves you like, when you want them. See also 'Rotation' in Chapter 2, pp.21-22.

WATERING

Rapid growth means regular watering in dry weather – say twice a week – and a good soaking when plants are larger. Remember that containers will need water even in damp weather, often into the autumn, but very little in winter.

PROBLEMS

Quality of leaves in summer can be improved by protecting with fleece or fine mesh to keep insects at bay, although a few flea beetles usually find their way in.

Caterpillars can cause significant damage, most notably to Chinese cabbage and pak choi in late summer and early autumn, so cover with fleece to protect them. Pick off and squash any caterpillars you notice, otherwise they can wander hungrily from plant to plant.

Slugs are a continual problem which must be addressed (see Chapter 8, pp.60-65), especially when plants are small and tender; Chinese cabbage, pak choi and komatsuna are their most sought-after victims.

The brown rings of fungal decay found on some leaves in later autumn are most common on older plants of certain kinds such as mibuna. Once they are infected, it is best to remove all damaged leaves and then keep picking small, healthier re-growth.

Sometimes plants wilt for no obvious reason, usually because the maggots of cabbage root fly are eating their roots. Fleece and mesh help to keep them out but damage is mainly confined to weaker plants.

Grey and white aphids are sometimes invasive on kale in winter and spring, mainly when there is little frost. I do not know a reliable remedy, but spraying with water will reduce their numbers.

HARVESTING

Leaves

The choice is between cutting and picking. Cutting works best in warm weather when re-growth is rapid, but the decapitation of baby leaves close to the plants' growing points means they take longer to re-grow; this is most apparent in cold conditions. Cutting works well for micro or baby leaves but is a one-off harvest when the stem is cut through.

For a longer period of picking through the cooler months of October to April I recommend carefully looking after your well rooted plants by pinching off leaves as they mature. 'Mature' means before they start to lose quality and develop brown fungal blotches as well as more slug holes. This applies to quite small leaves in winter, much larger ones in autumn and spring, so keep a close eye on your plants and maintain them on top form through good harvesting.

Oriental leaves are often shallow-rooted and you must take care in picking leaves not to disturb the fragile roots. Long thumbnails are useful for pinching through stems; or you can cut leaves singly.

It is definitely worthwhile picking off any old, discoloured and eaten leaves to make the harvest of new leaves easier, and to reduce hiding-places for slugs. Remove any slugs you may find, since just one can cause havoc in winter when re-growth is so slow.

Hearts

Red and white cabbage are often used in winter salads but here I am mostly concerned with Chinese cabbage whose pale, crisp hearts are deliciously juicy in autumn. They announce maturity by appearing much paler in their middles, and their outer leaves quickly begin to decay. They are more tender than ordinary cabbage and easily succumb to invasion by slugs, so it is best to harvest them as soon as they mature. Trim off all damaged leaves, and store in cool moisture, say in a polythene bag in the fridge, where they will keep for at least a month.

GENERIC / VARIETAL DESCRIPTIONS

Most of the headings in this section are species of plants. Because they are all slightly different vegetables, I include some specific sowing and harvest dates for each. Regarding varieties, I mention ones that are generally available and have done especially well for me.

Oriental Vegetables

Apart from one or two non-brassicas, such as mitsuba and edible chrysanthemums, all salad vegetables from the orient are members of the huge cabbage family. Their leaves are often faster-growing and more tender than the others considered here, but with no less flavour, and spicy mustard tastes are one of their characteristics.

Chinese Broccoli/Kale, also called Kailaan
Sow: August
Space: 25cm x 25cm (10" x 10")
Harvest: late August to October

This intriguing vegetable is worth a try, not least because its smooth and slightly waxy leaves resist flea beetle better than most others considered here. It grows fast, becoming quite large as small flower buds also appear. All parts of the plant are good to eat and extremely tasty – leaves, stems and flowers, although if you keep eating the leaves, there will certainly be less broccoli! The leaves are slightly firm and shiny, closer to European cabbage leaves than many oriental brassicas.

Chinese Cabbage
Varieties: *Wa Wa Sai* for small hearts, *Yuki F1* for larger hearts
Sow: July up to about 20th, or to mid-August for loose leaves
Space: 30cm x 30cm (12" x 12")
Harvest: September-October

Be warned – this is the most tricky vegetable that I know because it is the favourite meal of many garden pests. When I grew a couple in a bed of salad plants alongside twenty other different vegetables, it was the only one to suffer appreciable damage from slugs, which seem drawn to Chinese cabbage from far and wide. One of the plants somehow made a heart but its outer leaves contained several slimy monsters which were thriving in their moist, tender coolness.

Caterpillars are the other chief pest and a mesh or fleece is advisable from planting to about the end of September when hearts become paler and denser. They then tend to be infiltrated by slugs as age and decay set in, as well as being vulnerable to frost, so they are best cut by the end of October or earlier – see 'Hearts' above, p.121.

Sowing at closer spacings in August can give tasty, tender leaves until Christmas if the weather stays nice.

Komatsuna
Sow: late July-early September
Space: variable
Harvest: late August to October.

Komatsuna grows so rapidly that it often seems hard to find small leaves. Large ones are still tender, rather soft and watery and are good in stir fries. My preferred timing is to sow a few seeds in late August for leaves from late September and through October, when they grow more slowly. Watch out for slugs.

Leaf radish
Varieties: *Sai Sai* (green) and *Red Stemmed*
Sow: July to September
Space:15cm x 15cm (6" x 6") or 30cm x 8cm (12" x 3")
Harvest: August to October

Wonderfully mild leaves are produced in abundance by these fine plants, which are bred to be smooth and without the hairs normally found on radish leaves. Large seeds are easy to sow and fast to grow. Leaves grow large and darker coloured if left unpicked, and are also less tender. I prefer to pick medium-sized leaves frequently rather than cut all of them.

The radish root is thin and white (rose-coloured for the red-stemmed variety), edible but not especially tender, and is vulnerable to attack by cabbage root fly, so two or three sowings up to mid-September should ensure leaves from mid-summer to late autumn. Some plants survive frost but winter harvests are small, before improving briefly in early spring.

Mibuna
Sow: late July to September
Space: 20cm x 5cm (8" x 2")
Harvest: August to November

Named varieties are currently rare. Mibuna boasts a similarly rapid and many-leaved growth pattern to mizuna but has rather different leaves, dark green, smooth-edged, long and thin. They are best eaten small, so cutting plants at close spacings works well. By mid-October many leaves are often blotchy with brown fungi, but mibuna survives average British winters fairly well, making new leaves from late winter into April and some tasty flowering shoots as well.

Mitsuba or Japanese Parsley
Sow: June to early August
Space: 25cm x 25cm (10" x 10")
Harvest: July onwards.

Similar in name to mibuna and mizuna but a quite different plant; its other name gives a clue to its character. It is not a brassica and is related to carrots and parsley, of the *umbelliferae* family. The first difference you will notice is a much slower germination and growth is generally quite laborious at first. Late spring sowings may flower before making many leaves, but cutting their stem should encourage new leaves. Mitsuba is a hardy perennial and withstands frost, but prefers protection from an average British winter (see Chapter 19, p.184), and likes some shade and plenty of moisture in summer.

Mizuna
Varieties: are often unspecified; *Kyoto* is reliable.
Sow: late July to September
Space: 20-25cm x 5-10cm (8-10" x 2-4") – many spacings work, for different-sized leaves
Harvest: August onwards

The best-known and most flexible vegetable in this section, of extremely rapid growth and with juicy, mild-flavoured leaves, especially when young. July sowings are usually more holed by flea beetle and rise to flower more quickly than later sowings. Mizuna is good for cutting about 2.5cm (1") above ground level. If you thin seedlings out to about 20cm apart in each row, the remaining plants will grow large with long white stems. Harvest them by cutting across and above their base, removing all damaged leaves to facilitate harvesting the smaller re-growth of new leaves.

Mizuna looks pretty ragged through winter but if it survives there will be a few healthy, delicate leaves in March and early April, before the arrival of some tender, tasty flowering spikes.

Mustard

Varieties: mustards offer a most interesting range of leaves, with strong flavours and beautiful appearance. *Red Giant* is best-known for its ability, over a long period, to make new leaves which grow large and extra spicy if you don't keep picking them. The red colour intensifies in colder weather, becoming almost crimson after some frost. *Ruby Streaks* has more purple, longer and deeply serrated, feathery leaves, while *Golden Streaks* is similar but bright green, almost yellow in strong sunlight. *Green in the Snow* is the most frost-hardy and has pungently flavoured, oval-shaped, thin and slightly serrated leaves. I particularly like the *Streaks* varieties.

Sow: July to September
Space: as for mizuna
Harvest: August onwards

Harvesting the thin leaves of *Streaks* varieties by frequent cutting is easier than picking individual leaves, but wait until some leaves are about 15cm (6") long before the first cut. *Green in the Snow* lives longest while *Ruby Streaks* is usually first to flower. Many mustards can be kept producing over long periods by careful picking of larger leaves, but on the whole I find cutting these vigorous plants is effective.

Pak Choi

Varieties: *Tai Sai* for long leaves, *Green Revolution* and *Joi Choi F1* for short, fat ones.
Sow: late July to August
Space: 25cm x 25cm for larger leaves, 25cm x 5cm for smaller leaves (10" x 10" to 10" x 2")
Harvest: August to early October

Growing pak choi can sometimes feel like searching for The Holy Grail. It starts promisingly, has attractive leaves with thick white stems – and then is suddenly full of slug holes, or being eaten by caterpillars and flea beetles. I find it as difficult as Chinese cabbage but sow it more often because leaves are ready about four weeks after sowing in August, and young ones are delicious in salads.

There is a range of different-shaped and -coloured leaves of variable thickness, according to the variety grown. None are winter-hardy outside but pak choi can be reasonably productive in a greenhouse or polytunnel through the winter, as long as you are in control of slugs. *Tai Sai* is easier to pick with its longer, thinner leaves: all varieties can also be cut.

Tatsoi

Varieties: *Rosette Pak Choi* for compact growth, *Yukina Savoy* for longer stems
Sow: August
Space: as for mizuna
Harvest: September to October

Similar to its rhyming relative pak choi but usually smaller-leaved and more compact, with less stem. Shorter-stemmed varieties have lovely glossy leaves but are more difficult to pick; cutting is more realistic for them. Frost-hardiness is good and some reasonable leaves can be had in March and April, particularly if some shelter is given.

Rockets

Plant breeders and seed companies are feeding the growing interest in rocket with many variations on the main two types, which are larger-leaved salad rocket and thin-leaved wild rocket. They all grow in a similar way to oriental brassica leaves.

Sow: late July to mid-September
Space: 20cm x 5cm (8" x 2") sown in rows, or 20cm x 20cm (8" x 8") for multi-sown clumps
Harvest: August onwards

Salad and Wild Rocket

Salad rocket offers higher yields and milder flavours than wild rocket, with an increasing range of interesting varieties such as *Apollo*, which has larger and round-edged leaves, while *Skyrocket* has some qualities of both salad and wild, and is less easy to grow than ordinary wild rocket. The leaves of wild rocket are thinner, darker and more serrated, and its flowers are yellow rather than white.

Young leaves are the mildest, while older leaves on old plants can be hot and pungent. Flavour tends to diminish in winter when rocket comes into its own as one of the few plants to produce worthwhile amounts of new leaves, except in frosty weather.

Harvest by cutting or by picking larger leaves. Flowering stems will appear in early autumn from your first sowings but cutting them usually encourages plants to make more leaves. Flowering in spring is more persistent and leaf production diminishes to small amounts by early May, although wild rocket sometimes continues into the summer.

Kale

Although there are many kinds of kale, only a few have tender enough leaves to enjoy in salad, unless they are eaten as baby plants (see Chapter 4, pp.36-8 and p.40). Kale's winter hardiness and profusion of tender flowering shoots in spring are valuable assets.

Varieties: *Red Russian* is the only commonly available kale I know whose mature leaves are thin and tender enough to enjoy in salads. They are a pretty mauve colour with serrated margins. *Sutherland* is a hardy but tender-leaved green kale of fine flavour.

There are also, of course, plenty of insects that enjoy tender kale leaves, so it is worth netting or fleecing plants at first and also in winter if pigeons take over from butterflies as chief nuisance. I know that it may sound pretty boring to be always on the defensive, and in some years pests are not prevalent, but I am giving advice on the worst case possible. One August when I did not protect my kale, gall midges ate out a lot of the growing points and they ground to a halt, while the previous August had seen no damage.

Option 1: Spacing/growing for large plants
Sow: late June to mid-July
Space: 40cm x 40cm (16" x 16")
Harvest: October to May.

If your plants make it to autumn in good shape, you can enjoy some of the lower leaves, cooked if they are large, while leaving all small ones to fuel future growth. Medium-sized leaves can be chopped and eaten raw in winter. Then as winter draws to a close, new shoots with plenty of small leaves should appear at different points on the stem and by April these will be making flower buds. All of this new growth is delicious raw. Finally by May the new stems become thinner and tougher.

Option 2: Spacing/growing for baby plants

Sow: mid-July to early August more thickly
Space: 25cm x 5cm (10" x 2") or 20cm x 20cm (8" x 8") for multi-sown modules, for harvests from mid-August.
Harvest: August to May

Small leaves can be picked off from mid- to late August and regularly thereafter. Plants will be small going into winter but no less hardy for that and should provide more small leaves in late winter and until early May.

One bad pest in spring can be grey aphids that suck so much sap out of new leaves that they shrivel up. This happens particularly after mild winters just when plants look in good shape. Fleece is not an easy remedy over large plants; probably washing them with soapy water is the only answer and it is a rather tedious job.

Other brassicas

There are many other brassicas now available which make good salad leaves – certain kohlrabi, cabbages, turnip greens and texel greens are all tasty and of varied shape, shade and texture. Small leaves are the most tender and interesting.

Cabbages

Most leaves of European cabbages are a little tough and waxy for use in salads but see Chapter 4, pp.36-8 and p.41 for ideas on growing them as micro leaves.

Kohlrabi

Sow: July-August
Space: 20cm x 5cm (8" x 2")sown in rows or 20cm x 20cm (8" x 8") for multi-sown clumps
Harvest: August to November

Some kohlrabis have been bred for tender leaves, of green or purple hue, and they grow fast, but I have found them to be a favourite of many cabbage pests such as root fly and slugs. On the other hand, their leaves resist flea beetle a little, and the purple-leaved variety is worth a try for its waxy, almost translucent hues of purple and pink.

Rape

Sow: August to mid-September
Space: as for kohlrabi or closer, 15cm x 2cm (6" x 1") for baby leaves
Harvest: September to May

Like kohlrabi, rape is fast growing and like cabbage its leaves want eating small. It is especially suitable for growing as micro or baby leaves, or for sowing more thickly to cut baby leaves when young.

Texel Greens
Sow: July to September
Space: as for kohlrabi or wider, 30cm x 30cm (12" x 12") for large plants
Harvest: August onwards

A farmer once expressed amazement that I was growing Texel greens to eat, since he thought it was only good for pheasants, and it is certainly not well-known as a salad ingredient. Yet its leaves are tender, mild, fast-growing, and frost-hardy. When given more room the plants grow 60cm (2') high or more, with large leaves that are tasty as cooked greens and as resistant to winter weather as any other plant mentioned here.

Turnips for leaves
Sow: March–April or August–mid-September
Space: as for rape
Harvest: from three to four weeks after sowing

Young turnip leaves are pale green, hairy and tender, with a pleasant mild flavour. Closely spaced plants can be cut over two or three times and picking the odd leaf off turnips grown for roots should not discourage their growth too much. Also there are turnip varieties that have been bred for more leaves and less root, such as *Rapa Senza Testa,* and if allowed to grow large they will also do as tasty cooked greens.

May salad leaves with orache on top

Sugar peas – sown thickly for harvesting shoots

Amorina – July

Blood-veined sorrel on edge of bed

Spinach *Tarpy* F1 in pot – April

Red spinach *Bordeaux* – April

Radicchio *Rossa di Verona* – April

Lettuce *Nymans,* six months old

First harvest of carrots *Early Nantes,* sown in one of the salad beds – mid-March

Okahijiki – sown in May

Komatsuna on new outdoor bed

Lettuce *Freckles*

Beetroot in pots and growbags

Chapter 14

Spinach, Chard and Beet

Many colours, strong flavours

BRIEF SUMMARY

- *Leaves of strong flavour best picked small*

- *Sow spinach from February indoors and March outdoors, until August, best to avoid sowing in May and June*

- *Indoor sowings in modules are less at risk from slugs and woodlice*

- *Sow red, yellow, pink and/or white chard and beet in April, then one more sowing in June should ensure leaves until mid-autumn*

- *Spinach produces its tastiest leaves in the spring but is always at risk from slugs*

- *Chard is less delicate but still of interest to slugs*

- *Harvest larger leaves by hand or all leaves by knife*

- *Removal of flowering stems will prolong the useful life of plants*

- *Spinach sown in summer can survive winter to give a new crop of delicious leaves in spring. Chard is also reasonably winter-hardy*

Spinach, chard and beetroot all belong to the same family of Chenopodiaceae. They are descendants of wild sea beets which have been bred in different directions, chard for its colourful and fleshy stalks, beet for its roots and spinach for its more tender leaves. Spinach is often called 'Prince of Vegetables' in the Middle East, for its rich flavour and delicate texture.

In more recent times it has become common in Britain to eat these leaves in salads, when they are small enough to retain a mild flavour without the acidity and rather aggressive tastes found in larger leaves when raw. Chard and beets are mostly grown for the pretty colours of their stems and veins, compared with pale green colourations of the leaves in summer, turning darker in winter. I find that small chard and beet leaves rarely excite the palate, but spinach definitely can. Its flavour varies through the year, according to both season and weather, reaching a zenith of rich sweetness in the spring when it is most in season. Freshly gathered small leaves from young plants also possess a most pleasing succulence.

NORMAL PATTERN OF GROWTH

Spinach

A hardiness to oceanic winters and spring flowering means that seed is happy to germinate in summer and grow into plants large enough to survive the cold; it then grows again in spring and makes plenty of seed by early summer. Seeding can also happen in the same year and much more quickly from spring and early summer sowing. Regular picking of leaves in all seasons except winter will slow this process.

Chard

This follows a similar pattern but more gradually, so it needs sowing less frequently and each plant offers leaves over a longer period. Green chard or leaf beet can also be grown for baby leaves. Summer sowings which survive the winter will flower through the following spring.

Beet

Beetroot grown for leaves and regularly picked will eventually make a small root which is edible but tougher and less sweet than ordinary beetroots. As with chard, these roots flower after winter if frosts have not been severe enough to kill them.

SOWING

The main season of salad spinach – from April to November but with no leaves from June to mid-August – is covered by three sowings in February, April and late July. Chard requires only two sowings in April and June and beet only needs one sowing in April for continuous leaves.

When sowing direct, aim for about a seed every centimetre, two or three per inch, in rows 20-25cm apart (8-10"). Seeds are of a fair size and easy to handle. For indoor sowing, four seeds per module gives a good clump of leaves, plant at 15-20cm (6-8").

The earliest harvests from March onwards come from sowings made in late summer, between mid-July and mid-August; these also give autumn leaves. It is also possible to make early sowings of spinach in February in a greenhouse with gentle heat, then plant under fleece in late March or early April. Chard and beet are better sown later, in April and May, to reduce the risk of flowering. Then they should be cropping in June and July when spinach prefers to make a flowering stem.

GROWING

If seed comes up more thickly than suggested above, it pays to thin them out so that you have fewer, stronger plants rather than many spindly ones.

It is necessary to water in dry spells, especially spinach, whose tendency to run to seed in late spring and summer can be delayed for a while by keeping its roots moist.

CONTAINER GROWING

Spinach for small salad leaves grows well in containers and can also grow into large leaves. In early spring, for example, you can pick off its baby leaves for a month or so, when most appreciated, and then allow it to grow rapidly in May warmth – with plenty of watering – for a final crop of leaves to cook (see recipe in Chapter 10, p.80). Chard can be equally versatile and all the beets do well in containers.

PESTS

Slugs require continual surveillance and are easier to control when there is plenty of bare soil around. So keep on top of any weed growth, and remember that allowing plants to grow larger leaves, which offer shade and shelter, is more likely to result in larger numbers of slugs and more damage.

Some birds such as sparrows enjoy pecking holes in beet and chard leaves, which may then require the use of netting. Bird damage tends to show as many, even holes rather than the slug's more random and larger ones.

Spinach seedlings are a favourite meal of woodlice, which abound in many gardens and even colonise new beds and pots after a few months. Woodlice nibble the baby leaves at the centre of the plant, after which those leaves grow ragged. They make less impression on larger leaves so it helps to sow spinach in woodlice-free modules rather than direct. This should also help with slugs although if they continue to be a major menace, see the box on the next page.

HARVESTING LEAVES

Young leaves hold all the aces – tender, tasty, pretty – so it is worth picking regularly. A knife can be used to cut across the tops of plants, but always taking care to cut above the smallest visible leaf. The next cut will be ready a little later than when leaves have been picked off. Small spinach leaves are better picked than cut because of their more prostrate habit with leaves growing horizontally outwards, so that by the time you might have gathered them up to cut their stems they can have been carefully picked – although it does help to have a good thumbnail for pinching the stalk, to avoid root-disturbance.

A BETTER MOOD IN THE GARDEN

As well as harvesting all good leaves, it is worth removing any yellowing or eaten ones to decrease food and hiding areas for slugs. The appearance of the plant is also improved and this is psychologically important, helping to keep you enthusiastic and happy with your garden.

When flowering stems appear, keep pinching or cutting them to promote more leaf growth. The harvest can be prolonged over two extra months or more with chard and beet, but spinach leaves become smaller and more bitter soon after a flowering tendency begins, especially from May to early July, hence the need for more frequent re-sowing than chard.

Sometime in October growth will almost cease and although plants grow slowly through winter, there will be only a small amount of harvestable leaves until the arrival of some early spring warmth.

VARIETIES

This is a selection of varieties which have given me good results. There are many others worth trying and new ones are coming along all the time.

Spinach *Bordeaux*
This variety is tricky to grow because it seeds readily unless you wait until early August before sowing. However, the wait is worthwhile as its red-stemmed, pointed leaves are attractive and of good flavour.

Spinach *Galaxy F1*

Extremely fast to produce mid-green and rather pointed leaves, rising to flower quickly as well, therefore most suited to an early sowing for one or two quick cuts of baby leaves. *Galaxy* may also survive the winter from a sowing in early August.

Spinach *Medania*

One of the hardiest varieties for overwintering, but a little prone to being eaten by slugs. The dark, thick leaves are of excellent flavour raw, even when quite large and especially after cold weather, when the new leaves become impressively sweet. Best sown mid-July to mid-August.

Spinach *Tarpy F1*

An excellent variety for early leaves which are round and quite thick, dark green in colour and of fair flavour. A March sowing will normally rise to seed by the end of May.

Spinach *Tetona*

Slower to grow in spring than some of the earliest varieties and also longer lived, with slightly smaller leaves. A good variety for sowing regularly from April to July if you are aiming for continuity of leaves.

Tree spinach

An unusual variant, growing 60-90cm (24-36") high on a slightly woody stem, with many shoots which have glowing purple baby leaves at their centre. Leaves are also faintly purple on their undersides. Keep picking them, as larger leaves are tougher and better cooked, and the pretty young shoots readily run to seed.

Chard *Bright Yellow*

Yellow chard grows a little more quickly than ruby chard and has pretty, luminous stems which add zestful colour to a bowl of mixed leaves.

Chard *Rainbow*

As usually sold, this is a mixture of coloured chards from red to orange to pink to yellow to white, often with more of the pale colours which tend to grow more vigorously than highly coloured leaves. So if you want richly coloured chards, it is better to buy varieties of named colour such as *Ruby*.

Chard *Ruby*

Ruby chard is a selection of colour rather than a variety, but an increasing number of named varieties, such as *Charlotte,* are becoming available. All are usually about 98% true with dark red stems and veins and just the odd paler-stemmed plant.

Beet *Bulls Blood*
This variety has lovely dark stems and even its leaves are more ruby than green, especially in cooler weather. Sow in April and pick leaves until October or later, watching the baby beetroot grow as well! Unfortunately they are not sweet to eat because of continually losing their leaves to the salad bowl.

Beet *Red Titan*
Another beet with strikingly dark, crimson stems and thinner leaves than chards, but this variety does have some green leaf between its red veins and a good flavour.

Leaf Beet *Erbette*
Leaf beet has thinner stems than chard, of a pale green colour. *Erbette* has a better flavour for eating raw than most leaf beets and it survives winter a little better than most chards, with reasonable re-growth of pale green, quite fleshy leaves in early spring.

Chapter 15

Exotic Tastes and Colours

Small amounts of large flavours

BRIEF SUMMARY

- *Baby plants and shoots of many vegetables have appealing flavour, but avoid the poisonous Solanums – potato, tomato, aubergine, pepper*

- *Pea shoots are always popular: sow closer than usual and keep pinching out all growing points*

- *Broad bean plants can be treated like peas; their shoots have a stronger, less sweet flavour*

- *Other possibilities are young carrot tops, fennel leaves, celeriac, broccoli, asparagus*

- *Summer purslane is in its own idiosyncratic category of succulent, lemony, drought-resistant leaves*

- *For striking colours, try small leaves of amaranth, orache, red perilla and others from previous chapters such as red beet, lettuce and basil. See Chapter 4, pp.31-38 for more ideas on growing baby vegetable leaves in small spaces*

This chapter is about growing exciting tastes and colours from plants that are not difficult to grow. The yields of leaves and shoots are small but the flavours and colours are so vivid that only a small quantity is needed to give great character to salad dishes.

NORMAL PATTERN OF GROWTH

A wide range of plant types are covered here, so few generalisations can be made, except that peas, beans and orache will set seed by the end of summer, while many of the other vegetables will grow quite large if allowed to, with leaves that are too tough for salad. Regular harvesting at the right moment is thus important.

SOWING

Most of these plants should be sown between March and July and have special seasons when they grow best, so check dates for each one. Two sowings, early and late of any one vegetable, should give a long period of harvest because the same plants keep producing more shoots or baby leaves when grown as suggested.

HARVESTING

The quantities here are mostly small and regular. When you pinch off the top of a growing pea plant in spring it looks pretty terminal for the plant and for a while nothing more grows. Then the stem elongates and new shoots appear; harvest these and soon there are even more on several new stems – and so on.

Since most leaves for colour are of average flavour, sometimes strong and bitter when large, they are best picked small. This encourages plants to make more small leaves, and flowering is delayed over a long period.

CONTAINER GROWING

All plants in this chapter work in containers, and the coloured ones such as amaranth and orache look really attractive as well. Peas and beans require larger pots or tubs, because they can grow big and bushy after three months or more. Module-sowing works well for planting into containers, or when sowing direct you will need to modify the spacings a little as rows are not appropriate and closer spacings work well in pots filled with good compost. For example, the fennel spacing of 15cm x 5cm could become one seed every 5cm (2") in all directions.

PEAS

Almost any variety of pea can be used, but tall varieties have more vigour and their longer shoots are easier to pick. I grow mostly tall sugar snaps as I always save some of their seeds. I fear that not all pea seed which you buy is as fresh as it might be, resulting in poor germination, so I do recommend keeping your own if you have room in the garden to allow a few pea pods to dry on the vine.

Sowing

March is the best month for a first sowing, and you have until July to sow more, although late sowings tend to grow less vigorously and healthily in my experience. A well tended and regularly picked March sowing can last through the main season of pea shoots, which is May and June, while a sowing in May will give slightly less shoots through summer. Remember that mildew on the leaves can become prevalent after mid-July, depending on the weather and variety.

There are many ways of sowing pea seeds:

- Directly into soil: Either dib holes 2-3cm (1") deep and 15-20cm (6-8") apart, dropping three or four seeds in each, or draw out drills 25cm (10") apart and drop in about 25 seeds per metre (i.e. 1½" apart)
- In a plastic gutter of compost: sow peas every 2cm (1"), grow them under cover, then slide them into a shallow trough in the soil when of similar size to module-grown peas
- In containers outside: one or two seeds at an equidistant spacing of 10-15cm (4-6")
- Indoors: sow three or four seeds per module indoors in March for planting out after about three weeks when seedlings are 5cm (2") high, using the same spacing as above

Sowing indoors can help in safeguarding seed from hungry birds and mice. However, even in the greenhouse I keep a mousetrap primed all spring, because one rodent can eat a lot of potential harvests in a night.

Growing

If your garden or outdoor space is bothered by birds (such as pigeons and rooks) interested in eating or just pulling out young pea plants, you will need to cover plants with fleece or mesh for about a month, by which time the birds should be finding enough to eat elsewhere. Fleece will also help them to grow in cool spring weather.

Harvesting

When plants are 20-30cm high (8-12") pinch or cut off their top 5-7cm (2-3") and enjoy the early flavour of pea, with all it's promise of summer to come. You may then have to wait another fortnight or more before the next shoots are ready, and thereafter keep picking them at the length you most enjoy. Baby shoots are the most tender; longer shoots give more to eat and even their tendrils are edible, but a little tougher.

Eventually shoots will develop flowers of a lovely pea flavour, so you have many choices for different salads. Also if you are growing peas for pods, they often carry a surplus of flowers and the pea harvest will not be diminished by picking a few of these to eat. You could also pick their main, and then perhaps secondary, shoots once they are fully grown.

Conversely, peas grown for salading often manage to set a few pods on shoots which were missed, so a small harvest of peas can be enjoyed in summer as the production of new shoots slows down. New stems become thinner, spindly and rather tough after about two months of picking from the same plant. So pull them up for the compost heap and then, after removing your plants, there is still half the season left to grow another fine salad crop.

BROAD BEANS

As with peas, the growing tip of each plant is the initial harvest, but growth of new shoots is less prodigious and their flavour is less appealing – nicely 'beany' but also slightly earthy and powerful. A few flower buds sometimes come with the harvested tips and these are good to eat, offering a more delicate taste of broad bean.

Sowing

In view of the above I do not recommend sowing beans especially for salad harvests: if you do, space them at 15cm x 5cm (6" x 2"). Otherwise use your main crop which was, hopefully, sown in early November and survived the winter. Otherwise sow in February to early April, either directly or in modules, for a final spacing of 25cm x 5cm or 10 x 10cm (10" x 2" or 4" x 4").

Growing

Keep weeding and watching.

Harvesting

If you sowed seed exclusively for shoots, the growing point can be pinched out in May when plants are about 45cm (18") high. For harvests of pods, wait until May or June, depending on when you sowed, for plants to become covered in flowers and some baby pods at the bottom, then pinch out their growing points. New stems will often appear from the same roots and their growing tips can again be pinched out.

As well as giving you a tasty harvest, removing the top cluster of small leaves and flowers has two extra benefits: it encourages faster development of broad beans and makes it harder for black aphids to establish themselves, as they like to arrive and develop in the tight cluster of baby leaves if you have not harvested them for salad! The bean tops, lightly steamed, also make a tasty green vegetable.

Once pods are growing, plants put all their energy in that direction and new shoots become hard to find.

OTHER VEGETABLES' SHOOTS AND TIPS

This section is for regular pickings of shoots and tips – see also Chapter 4, pp.31-38 for sowing many of the same vegetables more thickly in seed trays for a quick harvest of tiny leaves.

ASPARAGUS

Not many people eat raw asparagus but I often snack on a spear or two when picking them and find quite different tastes and textures from those in the mild, creamy cooked ones. Chop two or three spears into small pieces to add crunch and flavour in late April, May and June.

BULB FENNEL

The extremities of the feathery fern-like leaves of bulb fennel are tender in salad and if you enjoy minty, aniseed flavours you will appreciate them. Bulb fennel is actually an umbellifer, like carrot, and its edible roots carry a noticeable taste of carrot. It is good value because all of the plant can be eaten.

Sowing
From May to August, direct in the soil at 15cm x 5cm (6" x 2") or at four seeds per module which are later planted at 12cm x 12cm (5" x 5").

Growing/Harvesting
Fennel is small and spindly at first, wait until plants are about 15cm (6") high before pinching out the growing point of a leaf or two and some feathery leaf edges. Keep picking for many weeks and then small bulbs will form and are good to eat before flowering stems develop, when plants should be pulled up.

CARROT

Carrot seedlings no more than 7-10cm high (3-4") have a surprisingly sweet flavour and are tender as well. Larger carrot tops have little hairs making their outer surface rougher, and fibres to stiffen their stalks. So if you want larger carrot leaves, I recommend using a hairless variety that has been bred for use as salad leaves and possesses, indeed, a fine carrot flavour – if you can find some seed.

Sowing

From March to August, direct at 15cm x 3cm (6" x 1") or four to six seeds per module to plant at 8cm x 8cm (3" x 3").

Growing/Harvesting

Early growth is slow but once plants are about 10cm (4") high, a few sprigs of leaves can be pinched off at intervals for a month or two. Roots will be small and barely edible when leaves are regularly trimmed back, also because of the close spacings here.

CELERIAC AND CELERY

The young leaves and leaf tips of these vegetables have powerful, bitter tastes which combine parsley and celery, see also 'parcel' in the next chapter. I do not recommend growing celery and celeriac especially for their leaves, but if they are in the garden anyway, a few leaf tips can be pinched as they grow.

SALSOLA also called OKAHIJIKI, KOMAROVII, LAND SEAWEED or LAND SAMPHIRE

A spiky, succulent plant of unusual salty flavour and crunchy texture, for eating in salad, shoots must be young and tender. They can also be lightly steamed or stir-fried, offering a mild flavour and unusual spiky texture.

Sowing

Sow from May to July, allowing about 15cm (6") between plants.

Harvesting

After six to eight weeks you should be able to pinch off shoots about 2-3cm (1") long. If plants are kept well watered they will then keep producing more of the tender shoots for up to two months. Eventually the stems become tougher as flowering commences.

SUMMER PURSLANE

This plant requires heat, sun and dry air, rather like basil. Therefore any moist, Atlantic summers, with the constant humidity and regular rainfall that is ideal for lettuce, are anathema to summer purslane, turning its round, succulent leaves to a paler than usual colour with much browning at the edges. However, a superb, somewhat lemony flavour and the crisp succulence of the leaves make it worth a try every year.

Sowing

Draw shallow drills for the tiny seeds and be wary of dropping too many in. Rows about 20-25cm (8-10") apart will allow room for plants to develop.

Golden purslane is best sown from mid-June to late July and crops for less time than green purslane, so at least two sowings are needed to provide leaves through July and August.

Green purslane can be sown between early June and early August, growing larger and cropping for longer than golden purslane if given a little more room. Three sowings in early June, July and August should give leaves for most of a hot summer.

Harvesting

When plants are about 10cm (4") high, the first shoots can be gathered, pinching all tender stems around the plants' edges. Shoots are normally about 3cm (1") long with about eight or ten leaves and a tender stem.

Then keep picking any new stems every few days – there will be noticeably more in hot weather. Watch out for seed pods which appear almost invisibly, hidden under some topmost leaves; they are the same colour as the leaves but possess a bitter flavour.

Golden purslane may crop for only three weeks before making bitter seed pods but individual leaves can still be picked for a while after that.

Green purslane produces tender new shoots for up to six or seven weeks, depending on conditions, and is higher yielding than golden purslane. Their flavours are similar.

TURNIP

In Britain this was probably the best known edible-leaf member of the traditional brassica family before the arrival of so many interesting plants from the Orient.

Sowing

Sow direct or in modules from March to mid-April and again in August to mid-September, using the same spacings as for carrots.

Growing/Harvesting

Growth is rapid and leaves can be picked or cut off once the first true leaves are formed; a month after sowing in spring and less than three weeks after sowing in late summer. Continued cutting of leaves will hinder root growth but if plants are thinned to about 10cm (4") apart after two or three leaf harvests some small turnips should eventually be gathered.

MICRO SOWINGS OF OTHER VEGETABLES

Many other small vegetable plants can be eaten whole for the flavours in both their baby leaves and tender, juicy stems. Cabbages, broccoli, parsnips, onions, leeks and others lend themselves to sowing in seed trays, window-boxes or whatever you can lay your hands on – see Chapter 4, pp.31-38 for more details.

PAINTING WITH LEAVES

Some plants have such a depth of pigment that their appearance amongst other vegetables can bring a fine touch of fiery exuberance and exoticism. I love to grow them as much for their exciting looks outside as for the colour lift they bring to bowls of salad leaves.

AMARANTH also called CHINESE SPINACH or BAYAM CALALOO

The many names of amaranth reflect its common uses across non-English speaking cultures.

Sowing

Amaranth likes warmth so wait until mid-May or June to sow, at similar spacings to fennel above. One sowing may do for the summer, or perhaps sow again in mid-July. If it is hot, there are larger leaves and a more rapid tendency to flower and seed.

Growing/Harvesting

Be prepared for quite slow growth in a cool summer, which at least helps to keep the leaves small. In warmth they become large and slightly leathery, less appropriate for salad with an unexciting, rather flat flavour. So keep picking the small leaves of striking colour – the variety *Garnet Red* has a gorgeous ruby tone to the underside of its leaves. Seeds produced at summer's end can be knocked out and kept for sowing, and are nutritious to eat – if a lot of work to prepare on a small scale.

ORACHE also called ATRIPLEX or MOUNTAIN SPINACH

These are many names for the same plant which is also known as 'red fat hen', an informative name, revealing its similarity to the well-known weed. Indeed if left to seed it will re-appear for years to come.

Sowing

Sow from March to June, using the same spacings as for bulb fennel above.

Growing/Harvesting

Leaves have a striking colour right from the beginning, and a few small leaves may be gathered when plants are only 7-10cm (3-4") high. Harvests increase steadily, and any flowering shoots can also be eaten when not too stemmy. Then after a couple of months or so the tiny flowers and seeds become more numerous than new leaves and the plants should be removed. One plant can be allowed to grow for seed, which takes about two months, and it may grow as high as 100cm (4'). Early sowings tend to give more leaves before flowering.

RED BASIL

For details on growing this see the next chapter, pp.145-148. I mention it here because the deep hue and density of its leaves stands out beautifully in a mix of salad leaves. Colour is my sole reason for growing it, as the flavour is ordinary and can even be bitter.

RED PERILLA

The dark red, crinkled leaves of this Japanese herb have both looks and flavour, but the latter is strong and spicy – not to everybody's taste in salads.

Sowing

Sow in May or June as it grows better in heat.

Harvesting

Keep picking small leaves from about a month of sowing and see how you like it!

Chapter 16

Herbs and Flowers

More exciting flavours and colours

BRIEF SUMMARY

- *Herbs are not difficult to grow, and enrich salads with deep reservoirs of flavour and nutrition, beautiful textures and some vivid colours*

- *Parsley is almost a year-round herb, but other annual herbs have seasons, so check for their best sowing times*

- *By careful picking you can prolong the useful life of many herbs and keep them producing tender leaves*

It has always puzzled me that the main role of parsley is as garnish, when it tastes so good and is full of vitamin C, especially when freshly picked. It is just one of many herbal possibilities for adding to salad leaves. A garden or patio with one plant each of parsley, basil, sorrel, coriander and chervil – but in different seasons (see below, pp.145-153) – can yield small and frequent leaves of rich flavour over weeks and months.

Flowers are another source of intriguing variety and colour, and not only the obvious ones like nasturtium and marigold. Some herb flowers have a wonderful flavour – garlic chives and coriander for instance – as do baby ornamental flowers such as heartsease and large ones like day lilies.

HERBS

NORMAL PATTERN OF GROWTH

The herbs covered here range from tender annuals (basil), which flower and die by season's end, through biennials (parsley), which flower in their second year, to hardy perennials (chives), which grow from the same roots year after year. Most of the flowers in this chapter are annuals which set flowers over a reasonably long period before and at the same time as setting seed, so many of them will grow again the following year from their own seeds.

SOWING

Both modules and small pots of about 5cm diameter work well for sowing clumps of herb and flower seeds. Set these clumps of seedlings into larger pots, beds or borders when their first true leaves are well established. Different herbs are ready to plant at different stages – check the descriptions below.

SPACING

Similar spacings work for many herbs; around 25cm x 10cm (10" x 4") for direct sowing in rows or 20cm x 20cm (8" x 8") when planting multi-sown modules. Multi-sown, module-raised herbs can be grown as unthinned clumps for harvests of small leaves, or thinned to individual plants at the spacings given for larger leaves.

BASIL (TENDER ANNUAL)

All basils are tender annuals, killed by even a slight frost. To grow good basil, remember two simple things: it needs warmth and dislikes too much moisture. Imagine it growing on an Italian hillside in full sun, and aim for a habitat like that in your garden!

In a wet British summer basil clearly struggles, and requires protection from regular cold rain: outdoor growing is a gamble, and succeeds only in hot summers. Otherwise, grow basil in a greenhouse, polytunnel, conservatory or even on the window sill.

With all these possibilities the fun begins because there are many delicious and pretty types of basil offering a spectrum of rich flavours.

Container growing

All plants covered here grow well in containers and can make you a nearly instant herb garden wherever is most convenient. If they grow more leaves than you require, it is better to keep plants on the small side by picking off and composting larger leaves. This keeps plants tidy, reduces slug numbers, means less watering and draws less nutrients out of the compost. Slugs can be an issue with tender basil, so avoid planting it before about mid-June in outdoor pots.

Sowing

Outdoor sowing is scarcely feasible unless you have great patience and can wait until summer's end for some leaves. Basil can be sown under cover from late April to early June, and baby basil risks rotting in soggy compost, so a heated propagator is an especially good way to get it going. Sow in a seed tray or two or five seeds per module. Be sparing with water as the tiny seedlings grow slowly unless it is unusually sunny.

Growing

When seed tray seedlings have two to four leaves, prick them out into modules or very small pots. Basil can be grown either as individual plants or as clumps of three or four together. Handle seedlings gently by the leaves only, so as not to squash their fragile stems.

Around a month or more after sowing, when your plants are 5-7cm (2-3") high, move them on to a slightly larger pot for another two or three weeks, at the end of which time they can be planted or potted in their final summer location.

One or more plants in a 25-30cm (10-12") pot can grow to a good size indoors and would probably be sufficient for most households. For this reason, it may be viable to buy the few plants you need, except that nurseries rarely offer many varieties, and you may miss out on the wonderful possibilities now available.

Harvesting

By the start of summer, from late June or early July, you should be able to gather a leaf or two, and then more each week as your plants become established. Watch for incipient flowering, when, in place of new baby leaves, you will see a stem and tiny flower buds, which can be pinched out and eaten. New shoots with growing leaves should appear just below its point of removal, then after a while they also will start to flower and should be treated in the same way. Soon you will have a small bush covered in new growth.

Each variety has different patterns of growth and best results come from closely observing where most new leaves and shoots are happening, then picking accordingly. Sometimes it is easiest to use a knife, for example with the small shoots of Greek basil which can be treated as though they are the extremities of a mini-hedge and trimmed accordingly, cutting about 1cm (half an inch) of new growth each fortnight or three weeks.

Through September there will be a gradual loss of leaf quality and occasional mouldy leaves and stems which should be put in the compost bucket. Keeping plants clean should help prolong their productive life into October, until it turns too dark and cool for healthy new leaves to develop.

Problems

Most difficulties in growing basil stem from cool, damp weather, which results in browning of the leaves, pale weak stems and a susceptibility to attack by slugs. Growing plants in good light and warmth, in fertile free-draining soil or compost without over-watering should ensure a plentiful harvest of healthy leaves. By early autumn it is difficult to maintain such conditions and the leaves and stems of the plant will gradually rot, so replant with a winter herb such as chervil.

Varieties

I recommend trying a plant of each, perhaps over a couple of years, for a taste of the exciting range of flavours and growth habits on offer.

Cinnamon Basil

Grows up to 50cm high, has good-sized leaves of spicy flavour and readily makes dark red flowers, which need pinching out regularly to ensure new leaf production.

Genovese Basil

The variety most used for making pesto from its rounded slightly shiny leaves which grow to a fair size in warm conditions.

Greek Basil

Makes a mound-like plant with masses of tiny light green leaves which can be shaved off in clumps with a knife or scissors. It makes a pretty pot plant and grows large if there is plenty of sun and warmth, and it shows less tendency to flower than most other basils.

Lemon Basil

The leaves live up to their name flavour-wise, are soft and tender and can liven up many salads or dishes of cooked food. A notable tendency to flower means that it must be regularly picked.

Lettuce Leaf Basil and Nufari F1

Lettuce leaf is one of the largest-leaved varieties but is quick to flower, and a new variety called *Nufari F1* grows very healthily and consistently, with equally large and mild-tasting leaves that are excellent in bowls of mixed leaves, or for rolling up around slices of ham, fish or cheese.

Lime Basil

The leaves of lime basil are smaller, firmer, glossier and more numerous than lemon basil, with an even more pronounced citric aroma and tangy flavour. With frequent picking it can grow into a dense bush of 40cm (16") or more.

Red Basil
This pretty variety boasts extremely dark ruby-coloured leaves, grows more slowly than most green basils, and has rather less flavour, sometimes with a touch of bitterness.

Sweet Thai Basil
Sweet Thai is a spicy variety, with hints of aniseed and cloves, and it shows a willingness to break out in colourful mauve flowers.

CHERVIL (HARDY ANNUAL/BIENNIAL)

Chervil is almost exactly opposite basil in terms of its climatic and seasonal requirements, as it thrives on dampness above all and dislikes too much bright sunshine.

Sowing

To have maximum leaves for least effort I recommend sowing in August to early September and growing the plants under cover through winter (see Chapter 19, p.180). Sow March to July for outdoor growing, bearing in mind that late July is often the best time for a long season of harvest. Slow growth at first makes module-sowing worthwhile: around six seeds per module to grow together in a clump.

Growing

Keep chervil's soil and compost moist; it enjoys shade in summer.

Harvesting

Keep picking larger bottom leaves or cut out sections of a multi-sown clump. 'Clear felling' across the top of plants about an inch above soil level will result in harvestable new growth in two or three weeks, as long as the weather is warm.

CHIVES AND GARLIC CHIVES (PERENNIAL)

These plants make perennial clumps of thin leaves which respond well to frequent harvests, either cutting or picking a few leaves at a time.

Sowing

Spring sowing works best, four seeds per module or small pot. Most springs thereafter you should have one or more established clumps and no need to re-sow.

Growing

When clumps are two years or older, they benefit from being divided in two or three with a sharp trowel, the root which is cut out being replanted in another pot or spot, for best health and vigour.

Harvesting

Chives often produce their first spiky, onion flavoured leaves before the start of spring, and they can be repeatedly cut or picked.

By May there will be several stalks of pretty mauve pom pom flowers. These can be broken into small, tasty florets, and then any unused ones are best dead-headed so that seeds do not shed everywhere.

Garlic chives produce flatter, garlic-flavoured leaves which can be cut from April to late autumn, and delicate heads of white flowers in August, which again are best either eaten or removed after flowering as a garden can soon be colonised by new plants.

CORIANDER (HARDY ANNUAL)

Sowing

This herb needs frequent sowing because it tends to flower after making relatively few leaves, except when sown in September and grown under cover through the winter. First sowings in March will yield leaves by early May for about a month, depending on variety.

A new variety called *Confetti* is slower to flower and also has rather different, more feathery leaves of fair flavour.

Harvesting

Frequent picking helps prolong the harvest and flowering can also be delayed by repeatedly picking off flower stalks.

If coriander flowers are left alone, seed pods will eventually ripen, turning brown and becoming hard towards the end of summer. They can then be harvested for cooking, although it is a fiddly job to shell them out of the seed heads, get a clean sample, pick out all the debris and blow off small bits of dust and debris.

DILL (ANNUAL)

The strong, aniseed flavour of dill is not to everybody's liking but it certainly carries an evocative suggestion of spring, with a heady, refreshing aroma as much as taste.

Sowing

Sow from March until July; early sowings will crop for longest, so a second sowing in May, third in June and fourth in July will provide dill from May to September. Sowing three to five seeds in a module or small pot works well. Any fallen seeds from previous years may well pop up unexpectedly and ensure that you always have a plant or two.

Harvesting

Pick whole leaves or some of their feathery tips and you can also eat the flower buds. Plants grow up to 60cm (2') high, and once flowers start to appear in earnest, they are best removed to concentrate on later sowings. Leaving one plant to set seed by the end of the summer is worthwhile.

LOVAGE (PERENNIAL)

Rich flavours of celery come from small amounts of leaf, while lovage seedlings are equally delicious and milder.

Sowing

In spring or autumn, in a small pot for planting out, or beg some root from a friend who might be dividing a large clump, or might have some self-sown seedlings.

Harvesting

Harvest at any time from about March to November; lovage is vigorous and will grow both tall and wide.

MINT (PERENNIAL)

Occasionally used in salads, in tiny quantities and chopped into small pieces. Flavours range from fruity applemint to spicy spearmint.

Sowing/Growing

Mint grows readily from small lengths of root and once established will colonise an increasingly large area, to the detriment of any less vigorous plants it encounters. So buying a plant or begging a piece of root from a friend is easier than sowing, and mint is best confined to pots and containers rather than being allowed to spread through beds and borders.

Harvesting

Keep pinching off the tender growing points of new stems and remove flowers for as long as you want to keep harvesting. Cut all dead stems back to near soil level at year's end, to make picking easier. Tasty new shoots appear as soon as the weather warms up in late winter or early spring.

PARCEL (BIENNIAL)

Of strong, metallic flavour, similar to the celery it is descended from. Used raw, a tiny amount of leaves is needed. Grow as for parsley below.

PARSLEY (BIENNIAL)

The most worthwhile herb to grow, of useful flavour and reliable, steady growth.

Sowing

Two sowings in March and July should supply leaves for more than a year, although there will be few new ones in winter when plants lie mostly dormant.

Seed germinates slowly, taking up to three weeks, and needs to be less than two years old for best results. But you need so few plants: three or four in a 30cm (12") pot, kept watered, should suffice for most households. Sow four to six seeds in small pots or modules.

Harvesting

Parsley can be cut but such violence is not normally necessary and large leaves are quite easy to keep pinching out. If in summer you have too many leaves and some are developing brown spots and yellow edges, it may be worth cutting all of them about 5cm (2") above soil level to allow healthy new growth within a couple of weeks.

Problems

All parsley is susceptible to aphids and to carrot root fly, both having the effect of turning leaves yellow and sometimes eventually of killing plants, mostly in spring and early summer – another good reason to make that second sowing in July.

Varieties

There are two main types, curly and flat-leaved. The curly grows more slowly and is often more hardy and long-lived. Flat parsley tends to flower by mid-summer from a March sowing but it has a slightly sweeter and more delicate flavour.

SALAD BURNET (PERENNIAL)

Sowing

Sow any time from April to July and I recommend just one plant for occasional leaves as I find its flavour disappointing, or rather its lack of flavour, and have not yet found anybody who enthuses over it. Leaves are also a little tough and chewy.

Harvesting

Plants grow large and offer plenty of leaves; aim to pick them as young and small as possible. Flowers are delicate white and pretty and seed in late summer and autumn. More plants can be created from root division.

SORREL (PERENNIAL)

SORREL VARIETIES

There are three main varieties, available as seed or plants:

- *Broad-leaved sorrel, which is the easiest to look after and regrows readily from 'clear-felling' with a knife*

- *Blood-veined sorrel, whose strikingly veined leaves are much smaller than broad-leaved, and suffer fungal damage in damp weather*

- *Buckler-leaved sorrel, which has tiny, tender round leaves that can be shaved off in clumps. It is harder to pick than the other two, especially when flowering on tough little stems which can become mixed up with leaves in picking, but the flavour is superb.*

Is sorrel a herb or vegetable? It has the strong flavour of a herb, and grows as fast as some vegetables. Broad-leaved sorrel is especially productive: its long, thin, pale green leaves look like spinach yet taste like freshly squeezed lemon juice. All the sorrels have a powerful citric acid bite which I use in small quantities to enrich bowls of plainer-tasting leaves.

Sowing

Sow from March until June; the early sowing can sometimes last through a whole year if it is not too hot and dry, especially if the dock beetles stay away.

Sorrel is perennial and makes an expanding, long-lived root which offers tender leaves as early as February in mild winters. I also sow new sorrel every year, as young plants have more vigour through the summer, whereas old roots are keen to flower in May and June and can take a while to make more leaves after that, unless it rains a lot.

Problems

Dock beetle's: these are round and shiny blue-green, laying clusters of bright yellow eggs on the undersides of leaves, quickly hatching out into hungry babies which make hundreds of holes on nearly all leaves. Three solutions are: to grow sorrel in raised beds or pots, where beetles seem less inclined to go; to harvest all leaves at one time, 1-2cm (½") above the ground, so that the beetles cycle of growth is broken; and to water frequently as beetle's dislike wet conditions, and sorrel loves moisture.

SWEET CICELY (PERENNIAL)

Of all the perennial herbs this offers the mildest flavour and the most tender leaves, as much juicy as they are herby, so it can be a larger component in bowls of salad.

Sowing

Seed is a little difficult to germinate, whereas small pieces of root can be cut off in winter and grown under cover in small pots for planting in spring, in beds or in a larger pot.

Harvesting

Keep picking new leaves from mid-spring until late summer when flowering means less leaf production, especially in dry seasons. Plants grow large if given space or in pots up to 30cm (12") diameter.

FLOWERS

More garden flowers are edible than we realise and I describe a few below. Nearly all herb *flowers* are tasty as well, including most of those mentioned above – chives, garlic chives, coriander and dill especially. I have also eaten chervil, fennel, marjoram and sage flowers and suspect that all herb flowers are fine to eat, if you enjoy the flavour of the herb leaves. There are also some lovely colours to play with, in the flowers of marjoram and sage for example.

Here is a small selection of the possible ornamental edibles, to which you may add others that you come to like:

BORAGE (HARDY ANNUAL)

Easy to grow from seed, so easy that gardens can fill up with it if seedlings are not hoed off sometimes. But the gorgeous bright blue flowers adorn almost any food and drink, and are prolific in summer from sowings in spring. A white strain of borage is equally prolific, but its flowers are less scintillating.

Sowing

From March to early August: simply scattering a few seeds is as effective as any other method.

Harvesting

Harvest flowers as soon as they appear, and even with regular picking there will almost certainly be some that set seed to ensure another generation of plants, usually during the next wet, warm spell of weather or the following spring, whichever comes first.

COWSLIP

Mild flavour at a time of year when salad is scarce, and easy to grow in the garden.

Sowing

Sow from May to July, direct or in small pots for planting out.

Harvesting

Harvest flowers the following spring and leave some to set seed: cowslip can be quite invasive in time as it grows readily from its own seed.

HEARTSEASE (VIOLA) (HARDY ANNUAL)

Another easy-to-grow flower and much smaller than borage, it hides away in cracks and crevices, thriving on poor soil.

Sowing

Sow at almost any time and once some plants have flowered and shed seed you probably won't need to sow it again.

Harvesting

Harvest and enjoy the flowers for eating and decorating, leaving the odd one to set seed for more plants later in the year or next spring.

LAVATERA also called MALLOW (HARDY ANNUAL)

An easy-to-grow plant with mauve and white striped flowers.

Sowing

Any time from March till July, plants sometimes survive through mild winters.

Harvesting

Flowering is prolific from about June to October.

MARIGOLD (HARDY ANNUAL)

Calendula Officinalis, of all the many different marigolds, is the most commonly eaten flower. It is also known as English or pot marigold.

Sowing

Sow from March to August for bright orange flowers, whose petals above all are nice to eat. It is another vigorous self-seeder so re-sowing will probably be unnecessary.

Harvesting

You can harvest flowers all summer, except in hot, dry weather when plants sometimes go dormant. Dead-heading old flowers makes new ones more likely.

NASTURTIUM (HALF HARDY ANNUAL)

There is a whole world of nasturtiums to play with. Flowers of many and varied hues are edible, likewise the leaves which range from dark red-green (*Empress of India*) to pale green speckled with white flakes *(Alaska)*.

Sowing

Sow in early May – no earlier because nasturtium is killed by frost. Seed can be sown as late as September when self-sown nasturtiums often appear during the first rains at the end of hot summers.

Harvesting

Harvest flowers and leaves all through summer if it is not too dry. Some are always missed and set seed for the autumn or following year. Cabbage white butterflies sometimes lay their eggs on nasturtium leaves and plants can be stripped bare by the caterpillars. Perhaps nasturtium can be seen as a decoy plant, attracting pests away from brassica vegetables, or perhaps it is just attracting more butterflies into the garden.

PEA FAMILY (HARDY ANNUALS)

Pea and sweet pea flowers have a lovely taste of pea and look fantastic in spring and summer salads. Sow as usual in late winter to mid-spring and harvest a few flowers as soon as they appear, leaving plenty to grow into peas or for decorative sweet peas, according to which sort you sowed.

TRAILING LOBELIA (HALF HARDY ANNUAL)

I sow some of this every April in the greenhouse and by late summer its translucent blue flowers are lighting up the garden. They will do the same for your salad too.

Sowing

Sow March to May under cover, in small pots or modules, for large clumps outdoors through late summer and autumn. A few will self-seed the following year but rarely grow to a good size because they usually germinate in June or July.

Harvesting

Harvest from July to October; plants are killed by the first autumn frost.

VEGETABLE FLOWERS

Be creative and try some different ones! For instance, only this year did I get round to eating broad bean flowers, and enjoyed their lovely scent and bean-like flavour. Many vegetables do not normally flower, as we eat them before they reach that stage, but all peas, beans, courgettes and squashes are worth a try.

Chapter 17

Outdoor Winter Salads

Difficult but precious

BRIEF SUMMARY

- *The main sowing months are August and September, check the details below for each type of salad*

- *Sow in weed-free soil or compost, because growth is slow and weeds often grow more quickly than these salads*

- *Expect small harvests*

- *Amounts of leaves to pick will vary according to weather*

- *Late winter and early spring sees a period of relative 'abundance'*

- *Flowers that follow this, mostly in April, are edible and tasty*

This chapter explains what can be grown for outdoor leaves in an average British winter. I use the word 'average' because some of what follows will apply neither in a much colder than average winter, nor in a much milder than average winter. Since, at the time of writing, the last two winters have both fallen into one of these categories, I am well aware of the uncertainties in planning to grow winter salad.

So bear in mind when reading this chapter that growing winter leaves outdoors is an inexact science with small and unforeseeable results. However, those results will be more precious because of that, and more highly appreciated than ten times the number of leaves in summer. I know this is true because why, otherwise, do I go out in bitter weather to hunt for a few leaves of lamb's lettuce? They really matter!

NORMAL PATTERN OF GROWTH

In a nutshell, to survive and then thrive through winter salad plants need to be both large enough to meet the vagaries of cold, storms and frosts and small enough to have the flexibility to temporarily 'shut down' in extreme weather.

A tricky problem is that one sows seeds in late summer and autumn at a time when the amount of 'growing days' is diminishing fast, but to an unknown degree. Unexpectedly warm weather in September and October can bring plants along too quickly before an unheralded severe frost in November that might weaken or even kill them. Or a cold wet October might see plants struggling to establish enough before a colder than average winter, when as a result they may scarcely make any significant new growth.

Erratic growth through winter is followed by a late surge in early spring with briefly plentiful leaves before flowering commences.

GROWING UNDER CLOCHES

These are an outdoor alternative to greenhouses and polytunnels, and although they do not match their yields, they work well for winter salad. Remember that they need pulling back or taking off for occasional watering, about once a month between November and March, more in April.

There are an increasing number of proprietary cloches on offer, many of them quite expensive. It is possible to make your own from stiff wire, if you are handy with pliers. My home-made, semi-circular hoops have a loop about 20cm (8") above the ends on either side which go into the soil. So when they are pushed in, on either side of a bed, the loops are at ground level and string can be passed through them and tightened above the polythene to the other side to hold it in place.

Best sowing dates in cloches are about a week earlier than those described in Chapter 19, so that plants are well rooted by mid-October. Treat plants similarly and remove slugs when picking leaves as they quite enjoy cloches.

Covering a bed such as those described in Chapter 3, pp.23-30 should give worthwhile pickings but it certainly involves extra effort to keep everything in order.

FLEECE

Fleece is prone to rip in winter gales and is less effective at trapping warmth when the sun is weak so I recommend it for spring rather than winter use. In March and April it can be used most productively to grow extra leaves on existing plants, as well as to bring new plantings into earlier production.

CONTAINER GROWING

Winter salads make an excellent use of beds or containers at a time when they are otherwise not needed. Use the sowing and planting times given to work out how you might slot them in with other salads and vegetables. If preceding crops are not finished before the end of September you need to raise plants in pots, trays or modules elsewhere, for planting by early to mid-October.

Some suitable preceding crops are summer lettuce, basil, carrots and French beans. Watering is rarely necessary in winter, although slugs can be a problem: I have had best success with rocket, leaf chicories and endives, land cress, winter purslane and chervil.

LAMB'S LETTUCE

This intriguing name may have originated from the shape of the leaves being similar to the form of a lamb's tongue, at a time when people were more acquainted with lambs' tongues than we are now. Another name for the plant is Corn Salad, possibly deriving from its wild relatives growing in autumn and winter stubble after the cereal harvests.

Like all winter leaves it makes a small plant which hugs the soil, hence the extra labour involved in its harvest. It also has a shallow root system to exploit the continual dampness of soil in winter and possesses a surprising ability to resist frost, considering how tender and juicy the leaves are to eat. They are also slightly waxy, with a somewhat buttery succulence that makes a pleasant change and balance to the fiery spiciness of rocket and mustard leaves.

Sowing

Any bare soil after summer crops is suitable, as long as it is not too weedy. Chickweed and grasses can quickly swamp slow-growing lamb's lettuce and involve plenty of extra time to control – mostly by hand-weeding in damp soil.

Normally lamb's lettuce is sown directly in shallow drills about 25cm apart with around four seeds per 10cm drill (10" x 1"). Seeds are light and blow around in the breeze so sowing is rarely exact; also it is often dry at sowing time so germination may happen in stages as soil receives autumn rains. Emergence happens slowly even in ideal conditions and the tiny seedlings take a surprisingly long time to get going in warm soil. This even applies to modules in a greenhouse that can be sown until late September.

Outdoor sowing for leaves in late autumn and winter is best done from mid-August to mid-September. Sowing earlier in the year is possible, say in March for cropping in May, and in July for cropping in September. However, lamb's lettuce does not like hot dry weather which frazzles its shallow roots, so early sowings are extremely weather-dependent: mild, moist conditions are the plant's favourite.

Growing

Once seeds are all germinated it may be worth thinning seedlings a little because harvesting in winter is a lot easier and more pleasant from a few larger plants than from dense rows of baby leaves.

In a dry September, plants may mark time and then put on a spurt when it rains, so watering is only necessary for earlier sowings. Keep on top of any weeds which may otherwise grow over the lamb's lettuce.

Because of the extraordinary winter hardiness of lamb's lettuce I grow it exclusively outside and see little benefit in indoor production, especially as it seems more prone to mildew when grown indoors (see below).

Problems

The lower leaves can be invaded by white, powdery mildew in warm and dry weather; and the best remedy if you see it is to water your lamb's lettuce, but plants that are once infected take a while to recover. The varieties listed below show less tendency to mildew than some others, in my experience, but are still vulnerable in dry conditions.

The risk of mildew is a major reason for not growing lamb's lettuce in late spring and summer. I did once try it and succeeded fantastically, because it was a freakily wet year, just showing how rules are made to be broken as long as you are aware of the risks.

Slugs are much less problematic than for most other salads and, although often present, should confine their attentions to decaying older leaves.

Harvesting leaves

It is a pleasure to watch the tiny rosettes of shiny green leaves enlarge into clumps, but they never grow beyond a certain size, depending on soil and variety. The central rosette of lamb's lettuce grows only to a certain size before its larger leaves start to yellow, at which point the main growth is of new rosettes at soil level, below the older growth above. So it pays to carefully cut the topmost rosette off older leaves, in order to allow more light to the young ones below, taking care not to cut too low, so that new leaf-clusters can grow out of the stem which is underneath your cut.

Secondary and tertiary harvests are usually a little smaller until more vigorous growth recommences with the arrival of milder weather in late winter, before small buds arrive in mid-April with tiny pale blue flowers soon after.

Varieties

D'Orlanda (also called D'Olanda)
This has pale green leaves of a good size and an ability to survive most British winters. I like its worthwhile yield and often space it at 20cm x 7cm (8" x 3") to allow for the extra growth.

Louviers
Dark green and extra waxy, medium-sized leaves.

Palmares
Quite dark leaves, grows a little larger than *Louviers*, smaller than *D'Orlanda*.

Verte de Cambrai
Probably the smallest of these varieties, more fiddly to pick but with firm and glossy leaves.

LAND CRESS

An extremely hardy plant whose dark green leaves are full of metallic flavour, similar to watercress but, not surprisingly, rather drier in texture.

Sowing

Sowings at any time of year may, in wet years, offer some good leaves before flowering. Otherwise, sow in July and August for autumn and winter harvests, and up to mid-September for picking in winter. Module-sowing works well; space at 22cm x 22cm (8" x 8"). Seed can be scattered in weed-free soils, or plants allowed to self-seed after flowering in spring, although land cress can become a little invasive.

Growing

Land cress grows a little more quickly than lamb's lettuce and purslane, but still needs careful weeding.

Problems

Land cress is hardy, but leaves are vulnerable to slugs and flea beetles if grown in warmer weather.

Harvesting

Leaves lie close to the ground and can be difficult to gather without lots of soil and compost. Some of the first leaves in autumn are quite large and worth picking individually; thereafter some cutting is easier, a few leaves at a time, but this is also difficult because one tends to cut into the quite long baby leaves at the same time as snipping off the outer leaves. If cuts are made too far from the middle of the plants long pieces of stem are left which eventually rot and get in the way of later pickings. Luckily, land cress leaves are strongly flavoured enough that you probably will not want to pick many at one time.

New growth in winter is minimal but should resume by mid-March and continue through April when the flowering stalks can also be eaten; they have a noticeably peppery flavour.

Varieties

Apart from ordinary land cress, the only variation I know is variegated land cress, whose leaves are extremely pretty, mottled with almost white patches; however, they grow more slowly and are fiddly to pick.

WATERCRESS

Watercress can be grown without running water, especially in winter when soil is so damp.

Sowing

Sow as for land cress, or earlier if you can keep it moist through any dry spells in autumn. Alternatively, place a clump of bought watercress in water or damp soil, where it should root and grow again.

Growing

If you enjoy DIY, you could follow the example of a friend of mine who has achieved several years of watercress in an old sink with a solar-powered fountain to keep the water oxygenated. Some soil or compost is good at the bottom – perhaps enough to fill a quarter of the depth of the sink.

Harvesting

Harvest by either cutting handfuls of stems or pulling individual leaves.

WEEDS

Certain weeds which are common in late winter and early spring are both edible and tasty. Hairy bittercress and shepherd's purse both have leaves rich in sulphur oils, making them bitter and invigorating. Chickweed is all edible, its little white flowers included, but has a dry and unremarkable flavour. Eating these weeds will both fill your plate and clear the garden of their invasive habits, as long as you clear them before any flowers have set seed.

WINTER PURSLANE

The correct name for this plant is *Claytonia*, and it has both differences and similarities to summer purslane. The delicious leaves are equally soft, waxy and succulent, round and dark green, but somewhat difficult to harvest and of variable quality. If grown without protection through a British winter, pickings will be small and occasional before tasty small white flowers in March and April. There is only a short interval between flowering and seeding and *Claytonia* can be quite invasive, so be wary of leaving it to grow and set seed in April and May.

Cropping under cover is more substantial – see Chapter 19, p.189.

Sowing

Sow in July and August. For sowing direct in the soil, use the same spacings as lamb's lettuce. Purslane also grows well in modules, a pinch of the tiny seeds giving a clump of several plants in each one, to plant out when the first true leaves are just showing at 22cm x 22cm (8" x 8").

Growing

Growth is quite slow and steady; keep well on top of weeds.

Problems

There are no major pests or diseases to worry about.

Harvesting

Purslane can be cropped as soon as it is holding a number of leaves, umbrella-style, above and around its slightly mounded core. By this time it may also be sending up a few small flower stems with pretty, miniature white florets. Leaves and flowers can be harvested individually but take

care not to upset the fragile root system and on occasions I have unfortunately detached whole plants. It is better to cut bundles of leaves with a
sharp knife: whole purslane clumps can be given a haircut, not too low
so that baby leaves closer to the middle are left to grow into a later harvest. In midwinter this may take a month or longer, or half that in
milder weather.

Harvesting finishes when the increasing number of flowers become
tougher-stemmed in early spring.

Varieties

There are no named varieties on offer at the moment.

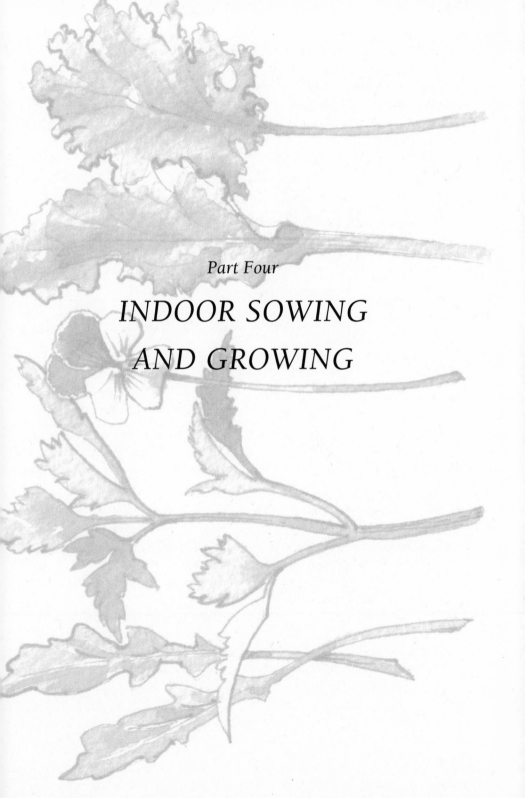

Part Four

INDOOR SOWING
AND GROWING

Chapter 18

Indoor Sowing

Earlier growth, stronger plants, more harvests

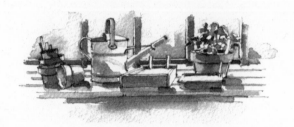

BRIEF SUMMARY

- *Sow indoors for more reliable results: less slug and insect damage to seedlings, less weather damage, and earlier crops*

- *Use different timings and techniques according to which salad you are propagating*

- *Module-raised plants can be used to rapidly establish succeeding crops, and to fill any gaps in existing ones*

A light space sheltered from rain and cold winds makes it possible to reliably raise plants at any time of year, especially in late winter and spring. It can increase the productivity of a garden out of all proportion to its small size. Having some healthy plants ready to fill gaps at particular times helps to ensures a steady supply of leaves through the year.

Chapter 6 has general details of suitable structures, modules and composts to use. Indoor plant-raising can be fun but remember that plants need regular water – every day in sunny weather – especially when they are larger and nearly ready to go out. Seed trays need less watering but involve either pricking out of their seedlings, or thinning them out to grow on. This chapter offers some precise details, with plenty of sowing ideas.

PLANT TRAYS

Most plant trays are made of plastic, and while it is an excellent material for holding compost and moisture, there are also problems of waste and landfill. However, many gardeners do not realise that it is safe to reuse seed and plant module trays and pots without even washing them, and definitely without using disinfectant. All of my seed and module trays have never been cleaned and have been used to raise healthy plants for two decades, provided they were sturdy in the first place.

So buy the best quality you can find and keep reusing them. Some plastics are now recyclable but repeatedly raising plants in the same trays and pots is a far greener practice.

Seed and plant trays come mostly in A4 and A5 sizes and can be filled with many different kinds of plants at one time. If you buy plants, they often come in useful containers which can be reused.

Modules come in various sizes. As a rule of thumb, forty to an A4 size tray is good for larger plants and sixty per tray for smaller plants. If possible fill with organic multipurpose compost; see *Resources*, pp.192-3 for suppliers.

Plastic module trays are quite cheap and often rather brittle. However, careful use will see them endure a few seasons, although their base may be damaged in pushing plants out. Thoroughly watering trays of young plants before planting helps with this.

You may also see 'insert trays' offered, and I recommend avoiding these as they seem designed to self-destruct in extracting plants from their flimsy plastic.

Polystyrene trays are more sturdy and plants seem to like them. I have some that are over twenty years old, missing their corners but otherwise alright. Compost needs to be pushed into them firmly. When the root structures of the plants are sufficiently developed to hold the compost together, they are quite easy to push out through the large holes in their bottoms.

SOWING

Seed trays and module trays of forty to sixty holes can be sown with different seeds at the same time, for eventual planting out together, although different growth rates mean that some may be a little under- or over-mature. Have a look at the seasonal example of module-sowing on pp.169-70 to gain an idea of what can be sown together.

MAIN MONTHS FOR SOWING INDOORS

This chart is based on the salad seasons and gives a brief outline of the best times to sow different salads with **number of weeks** from sowing to planting out.

	LATE JAN or FEB	MAR	APR	MAY	JUN	JUL	AUG	SEPT
VEGETABLE	WEEKS TO PLANTING							
Basil				10	6 to 8	6 to 8		
Chard		6	5	4	3 to 4	3 to 4	3 to 4	
Chervil							5	
Chicory				5	4	3 to 4	3 to 4	
Coriander		6	5	4	3 to 4	3 to 4		
Dill		6	5	4	3 to 4	3 to 4		
Endive				5	4	3 to 4	3 to 4	
Kale						2 to 3	2 to 3	
Lamb's lettuce							4	5
Land cress							3	3
Lettuce	7 to 8	6 to 7	6	5	4	3 to 4	3 to 4	
Mizuna	5						2 to 3	2 to 3
Orache		6	6	5	5			
Oriental leaves						2 to 3	2 to 3	2 to 3
Parsley	11	9	8	7	6	6		
Peas	5	4	3	2 to 3	2 to 3	2		
Radicchio						4 to 5	4 to 5	
Rocket						2 to 3	2 to 3	2 to 3
Sorrel	7	6	5 to 6	5	4 to 5	4		
Spinach	5 to 6	5	4 to 5	4	3 to 4	3 to 4	3 to 4	
Spring onions	8 to 9	7	6	4 to 5	4	4		
Winter purslane							3	3

These numbers are a guideline only, and will vary from year to year and according to the warmth of your propagating facility and size of pot or module used.

Basil *Cinnamon*

Seed tray of winter salad: kales, chicory, endive and sorrel – 8th February in greenhouse

Mibuna, mizuna, rocket and leaf radish in greenhouse – 5th December

Rocket and mustards in mushroom tray – 8th February in greenhouse

Chicons being forced in house cupboard – January

Lettuce in greenhouse – 8th February, many leaves harvested

Tatsoi *Yukina Savoy* in tunnel – February

Claytonia in tunnel – February

Parsley in tunnel – February

Land cress in tunnel – February

Rocket *Apollo* in tunnel – April

Abundance of mustard *Golden Streaks*

Mustard *Ruby Streaks*

Lavatera & marigold – September

Nasturtium *Alaska* – September

SOWINGS TO PROVIDE A MIX OF SALAD LEAVES FROM MAY TO NOVEMBER

This programme of sowing is **to provide a daily mix of many different leaves** over at least six months, as long as the plants are regularly picked over and are well looked after. If you want different herbs, choose them from the table of dates on the opposite page. The later sowings provide plants to fill gaps after early sowings have finished cropping, for example leaf endive after spinach and radicchio after peas.

- February: lettuce, spinach, peas, parsley, coriander
- March: sorrel, chard, dill, orache
- Mid-May: lettuce, leaf endive and chicory, basil
- Early July: radicchio (or could be late July for smaller hearts)
- Late July: lettuce, hearting endive, spinach
- From early August: rocket, any of oriental leaves, winter purslane, land cress
- Early September: rocket, lamb's lettuce, mizuna, mustard

FOUR SOWINGS FOR THE FOUR SEASONS

Here is a seasonal example for one or two forty-hole A4-sized module trays – a slightly simpler programme with just four sowings. Seed trays could also be used in the same way, although planting out is a little more tricky. You could also vary the total amounts according to the size of growing area and the module numbers according to your preferences. Numbers refer to module compartments sown, not seed used – check below to see which salads can be multi-sown. As far as possible I have grouped fast- and slow-growing plants in the same trays.

For planting out, these plants require a growing space of about 3m x 1m (10' x 3'). If after planting a few are left over, keep them in reserve to fill any gaps arising from slug damage. With regular picking, if they all grow well, they should yield enough leaves for four to six people between May and September, and smaller amounts after that.

March (2 trays)
First tray: 27 leaf lettuce of different varieties, 6 spinach, 3 sorrel, 2 chard, 1 coriander, 1 dill. Second tray: 12 pea, 8 mizuna for a half tray of fast plants; and 14 spring onion, 4 parsley, 2 orache for a half tray of slow plants.

Late May (1 tray)
30 leaf lettuce, 3 leaf endive, 3 leaf chicory, 2 chard, 2 dill.

Mid-July (2 trays)

First tray: 24 leaf lettuce, 16 radicchio (for hearting, early and late varieties). Second tray: 6 rocket, 6 kale, 6 mustards, 4 pak choi, 6 frizzy endive, and for hearting: 8 scarole endive, 4 sugarloaf.

Early August (2 trays)

10 rocket, 10 mustards, 10 leaf radish, 10 mizuna or mibuna. Also 8 leaf chicory (mixed), 8 spinach, 8 leaf endive, 5 land cress, 5 winter purslane, 4 chervil, 2 chard.

SEED RATES AND TOP TIPS FOR MODULE- & POT-SOWING OF EACH SALAD

Check the chapters on different salads to be clear about which kind you want; for instance whether it is endive for hearting or for loose leaves. The point here is to grow the number of seedlings in modules and pots you want as clumps in the ground. Each module is planted out intact, with no thinning except to pinch out seedlings where too many seeds were dropped in by mistake. I urge you not to disentangle the roots of plants growing together in one module.

Amaranth

Fast to germinate in summer warmth, sow a pinch of about six seeds per module.

Basil

The most difficult salad plant to raise, needing sufficient heat and not too much moisture when small. Up to five seeds per module should see three plants in a clump, while one plant per module makes for good pickings over a long season.

Chard

Some chard seeds grow more than one plant but four seeds per module is about right, to grow smaller plants for salad leaves.

Chervil, Coriander, Dill

All these herbs grow well in a clump so four or five seeds per module is good; if you want thicker stems, sow two seeds only.

Chicory for hearting (radicchios)

Reliable germination means that two seeds per module, later reduced to the single strongest seedling, is usually effective.

Chicory for leaves

Sow about five seeds per module to have plenty of small leaves per clump at picking time.

Endive for hearting

Sow two seeds per module and thin to one seedling after a week or ten days.

Endive for leaves

Sow three to five seeds per module, depending on how large you want leaves to be.

Kale

Sow up to six seeds per module to have small leaves for cutting. See also pp.126-7 for the two different sowing options.

Lamb's lettuce

Grows slowly and germination is not always good; try four seeds per module and be patient.

Land cress

Two or three seeds per module, thinned to one, will give plants with larger leaves for easier picking.

Lettuce

Germination is usually excellent, so one seed per module often gives a 90% success rate. Lettuce also grows well after being pricked out from a seed tray. Cover seed with only a dusting of compost and keep germinating seed sheltered from sun in hot weather.

Orache

Up to six seeds per module or small pot; one such clump should provide plenty of leaves.

Oriental leaves

Most of these grow well from four or five seeds per module, except for Chinese cabbage to make hearts which needs two seeds, later thinned to one plant per module.

Parsley

Slow to germinate; sow two to five seeds per module, depending on whether you want large or small stalks of parsley.

Peas

Three or four seeds per module will give a productive clump of pea plants.

Purslane

The seed is tiny; one pinch of four or five per module works well.

Rocket

Four or five seeds per module give clumps of plentiful, medium-sized leaves.

Sorrel

Thickly sown is best for small salad leaves, so about six of the tiny seeds per module is good.

Spinach

Four seeds per module will ensure growth of more small leaves, rather than fewer large ones.

Spring onion

I grow these in clumps of up to eight onions, so ten seeds per module is my normal practice. Sow deeper than other seeds, under up to 1cm (½") of compost.

HOW BIG A PLANT?

Seedlings will grow readily into young plants, whose eventual size depends on the compost and on how much of it is available to them. A key signal of plant growth stopping is when their lower leaves – especially the ground-hugging cotyledons – start to turn yellow, indicating that most nutrients in the compost have been used up. How long this takes depends on the compost quality and the plant's speed of growth; experience will help you assess when to expect it.

As plants start to run out of nutrients, they also seem to toughen up a little as their leaves become less lush and more fibrous. So as soon as they look a little pale, harden them off outside and they will then be fine to plant out.

If over-grown they may become diseased. For example, lettuce leaves can pick up mildew on their undersides when they become overcrowded in modules, although this will eventually disappear after planting out.

WATERING

This simple act is vitally important for successful plant-raising. It is a basic practical task, needing good observation above all. Learn to know the look of dry compost as it cracks away slightly from edges of modules, trays and pots, and to recognise plants that are dry, whose leaves turn a slightly darker colour and become matt rather than shiny. Try to water enough that you see this infrequently!

The opposite problem of over-watering is most common on baby seedlings whose leaves are not transpiring much water and their stems may rot if over-watering persists. In dull, cool weather you should be watering a third to a half as much as on sunny days. Just keep watching those plants, gradually watering them more as their leaves enlarge.

PESTS

Slugs

Always be vigilant for slugs and snails, because if they are not removed at the first sign of damage, large amounts of potential harvest can quickly disappear.

Firstly, clean out whatever structure you are using before sowing, looking under any objects lying around and sweeping out the dark corners. Then you should be in the clear for a while, but if *ever* you notice any eaten leaf, check immediately underneath seed or plant trays, the staging, a crevice in the door frame and anywhere a little damp and sheltered from the sun, where a slug or snail will be digesting those leaves and whence they will surely re-emerge.

Woodlice

Woodlice also can damage young seedlings by nibbling their stems and baby leaves, and are more difficult to control because of their large numbers. A good sweep out of the propagating area before starting sowing will certainly help.

Ants

Ants love warm, dry conditions and are difficult to dislodge once established. I have flying ants in my sandy propagating bench and have not managed to deter them with boiling water, the most commonly suggested remedy. Now I place thin wooden battens on top of the sand in summer, after the propagating heat is turned off and when the ants are most active, to keep seed trays and modules suspended above the sand, which keeps the ants from entering compost from the bottom, where they otherwise discourage growth with their acidic secretions.

Chapter 19

Salad Leaves through the Winter

Growing indoors

BRIEF SUMMARY

- *Choose your favoured flavours from the descriptions given*
- *Sow mostly in September, plant in October after tomatoes and other summer crops*
- *Look after plants with careful and regular picking to keep them producing until spring*
- *New leaves are relatively small and scarce in midwinter, more substantial by March and abundant in April*

Not only is winter much enlivened by salad leaves, but some of the prettiest leaves and best flavours grow only in winter months. The ones described in Chapter 17 grow outdoors, but to expand the repertoire and the quantity of leaves, you need a covered space which is in at least half sun to make the most of those precious golden rays.

Well cared for winter plants will then surge ahead in early spring, from late March to early May, at a time when few outdoor leaves are ready and just when some bowls of fresh leaves are most welcome.

GROWING SPACES

Polytunnels

Tunnels are good for winter salad but are cold at night and growth is usually slow from Christmas to early February. Then in mild springs you may be overwhelmed by the abundance of leaf growth!

Greenhouses

These have greater warmth than tunnels because glass holds more warmth at night than plastic and admits more light, so greenhouses allow more consistent growth. Plants can be grown in a bed of soil with compost added, or on staging in compost-filled containers of any kind, such as old fish or mushroom boxes made of wood or polystyrene.

Conservatories

These are warmer again, but suffer lower light levels because of house walls and this makes quite a difference in midwinter.

CONTAINER GROWING

Containers or pots of salad can be brought into a conservatory or greenhouse in November (see above). Salad leaves seem happy in any kind of box, tray or pot. Larger, deeper containers result in more pickings, as plants can root more extensively and keep producing healthy leaves over a long period. Come the spring, containers can be moved outside and planted with different kinds of salad; before doing so, it is best to renew a little of their compost and to reinvigorate the rest, see Chapter 4, p.33.

Plant spacing in containers will be closer than those recommended here and baby leaves can be grown through the winter in boxes and trays, again see Chapter 4.

FLAVOURS

Many winter salads have stronger flavours than summer leaves, making them a good tonic for dark, cold days. Mustard leaves, for example, are hot and peppery and best eaten in small amounts.

One of the more frost-resistant salad plants is leaf chicory, although its flavour is rather bitter and not to everybody's liking. Even so, chicory leaves complement the more fiery mustard leaves and can be transformed with a sweet dressing which creates a lovely balance of smooth bitter-sweet tastes.

With a little planning and careful picking it is possible to have an extraordinary range of taste in the winter salad bowl. Before sowing, check the information given on pages 178-89 on flavours, to be sure of having the ones you want.

SOWING

Autumn

Because of rapidly shortening days in autumn, sowing dates are more precise than in spring, when plants of later sowings have more chance of catching up with those sown earlier; whereas in September and October, a week's difference in sowing date will be apparent for a long time as plants run out of light and warmth. Follow the dates given as much as possible, and sow a little earlier in northern Britain.

Winter

If you still have empty gaps in midwinter, they can be filled by sowings after about mid-January if it is not too cold, but it will take longer than in the autumn for harvestable leaves to grow. Fast-growing brassicas such as leaf radish are good for winter sowing. Early March sowings of mizuna, pak choi, spinach and leaf endive can also create abundant harvests of leaves in April and May.

SPACING

Longevity of harvest is closely linked to distance between plants or clumps of plants: 22-25cm (8-9") allows room for roots to develop over the whole season. Using this spacing also means there will be some clear soil around all plants, helping to discourage slugs.

CARE OF SALAD PLANTS IN WINTER

Once established, winter salad plants under cover, correctly spaced, can produce leaves for five or six months, even more in a few cases. So look after them well, mainly by careful picking of leaves on a regular basis – although this may be as little as fortnightly in frosty midwinter weather. By spring they will seem like old friends and repay your conscientious attention with amazing harvests.

Watering is much less regular than in summer and is best done weekly at most, to allow surface soil and compost to dry out in between. Slugs and mildew are thus discouraged. Water more frequently as winter turns to spring.

HARVESTING LEAVES

As well as regularly picking the leaves you want to eat, have an eye for the health of your plants and keep removing any frost-damaged or diseased leaves. This makes it easier to pick leaves the next time, gives less cover to slugs and yields a further important advantage – they grow better! My experience suggests that plants feel better about themselves when kept looking nice, and we feel better too when caring for a healthy-looking growing space. A virtuous circle of gratitude is created, benefiting us and the plants.

AFTER HARVESTING

As winter salad plants rise to flower in the spring you can follow them with exciting summer crops such as tomatoes, melons and peppers. I recommend these rather than planting more salad, to limit any build-up of pests and diseases.

SOIL CARE

If growing in soil in your greenhouse or polytunnel, there is absolutely no need to dig it at any stage. Spreading 50-75cm (2-3") of compost in May, before planting *summer* crops, will provide sufficient nutrients and soil health for them *and* for winter salads planted in October. By autumn the compost will have been partly taken in by worms and the soil/compost surface should be soft, crumbly and mostly bare of half-rotted fibres – just right for tender salad plants.

PROBLEMS

See Chapter 8 for many tips on keeping slug numbers down: the golden rules are check for slugs before planting, remove any weeds, keep some bare space between plants and regularly pick small leaves.

Aphids may appear in spring but should not become too numerous if you are watering enough and they can easily be washed off leaves after picking.

Frost should not damage the plants described here unless it is abnormally severe – say -10°C (14°F) or colder. Again, picking helps because small leaves resist frost better than large ones.

SALAD LEAVES FOR INDOOR GROWING IN WINTER

CHARD

Flavour

Not the most tasty leaves, rather acid and tannic, but their prettiness adds quality to the mix. Few plants are needed.

Varieties

Grow the colours you fancy, from ruby to pink to yellow to white. Paler colours grow faster, darker colours are accentuated in midwinter.

Sowing

Any time in September, depending when you want to start picking leaves. Early September sowings start producing by about mid-October, late September sowings by November or December.

Module-sowing

Four seeds.

Spacing

As close as 10-15cm (4-6") will give small and numerous leaves.

Leaf growth and picking

Chard survives frost well by turning a deeper colour in cold weather, losing some of the bright green part between its veins. Keep pinching off the outer, dark leaves to eat, then in February and March they will become greener and more frequent, larger and fleshier. By late April or early May plants will show signs of flowering but can be kept going if you pinch out the tops of any stems. New small leaves will then appear lower down on these stalks.

CHICORY

Flavour

Rather bitter, less so in cold weather

Varieties

There is a range of leaf shapes and colours, see Chapter 12, pp.111-14 for more details. For ease of picking I recommend *Catalogna Gigante da Chioggia* with its long leaves and *Red Ribbed Dandelion*, of similar habit but with an attractive dark red stalk.

Sowing

September to early October.

Module-sowing

Four seeds is plenty.

Spacing

22cm is fine.

Leaf growth and picking

Stems of the longer-stalked varieties can be repeatedly twisted off or pinched out near soil level as they grow to the size you want. If you cut across the top of plants, re-growth will take longer. By April you may have too many leaves, so repeated cutting can be worthwhile. Flowering stems appear by late April and picking or cutting them out will prolong growth.

ENDIVE

Flavour

Only slightly bitter in cold weather, plenty of 'green' taste.

Varieties

A leaf endive such as *Riccia Romanesca da Taglio* (also known as *Romanesco*) grows longer leaves that are easier to pick and perhaps a little more bitter in flavour. Scarole and frizzy endives (see Chapter 12, pp.109-111 for varietal detail) can be grown and picked as for leaf lettuce but are best not allowed to heart up as they are then more vulnerable to frost, until March at least. *Bianca Riccia da Taglio* has pretty yellow colour and a mild flavour.

Sowing
September to early October

Module-sowing
Up to four seeds but one for scarole types.

Spacing
Standard 22cm.

Leaf growth and picking
Early pickings of small leaves between November and February can be fiddly, especially when leaves lie close to the soil. If you persevere and keep plants tidy, removing any rotten leaves after hard frosts, there should be some lovely new growth in March, April and into May. Regular picking in these months will delay flowering.

HERBS

Flavours
A wide range of stimulating possibilities, from the pungency of coriander to the spiciness of chervil.

Types
Flat- and curly-leaved parsley, mitsuba, coriander and chervil are four main possibilities; all resist frost and grow vigorously in March and April.

Sowing
July or August for slower-growing parsley and mitsuba, August or September for chervil and September for coriander.

Module-sowing
Between one and four seeds, depending on whether you want smaller or larger stalks.

Spacing
22-25cm (up to 10") allows room for plentiful leaves.

Leaf growth and picking
Much depends on the winter, and coriander may succumb to severe frost, while chervil, of all these herbs, should keep producing small stems. By March there will be a noticeable difference as plants enlarge and leaves

take on a dark, healthy lustre, so keep picking hard, to encourage healthy new growth. Flowering will occur from sometime in April and can be postponed by continual picking of flower stems.

KOMATSUNA OR MUSTARD SPINACH

Flavour
Younger leaves are especially mild, while there is more turnip flavour and some pepper in older leaves. All are tender.

Varieties
In Britain it is usually offered simply as 'komatsuna'.

Sowing
Mid-September to mid-October.

Module-sowing
Four or five seeds per module.

Spacing
Standard 22cm.

Leaf growth and picking
One of the fastest-growing vegetables, hence its mild flavour, but also seriously prone to slug damage, enough to make me suggest you avoid growing it unless your space is slug-free. It resists low temperatures well. Keep picking unless you want large leaves for stir-fry, while the flowers in early spring are tasty raw or lightly cooked.

LAND CRESS

Flavour
Strong, bitter, somewhat acid – best diluted with milder leaves.

Varieties
Ordinary green, or variegated which can be prettily white in patches.

Sowing
September to early October; seed is small and quite slow to grow initially.

Module-sowing

A pinch of seed – two to four plants is good for picking.

Spacing

Standard 22cm.

Leaf growth and picking

Leaves on young plants, especially in midwinter, lie flat to the soil; a little tricky to twist off. By early March there is stronger growth and leaves become a little more upright, and are much more numerous by April, when stems with small yellow flowers appear. These can be eaten and removing them will encourage more leaf growth, especially of the variegated cress which I have managed to keep going all summer and beyond.

LEAF RADISH

Flavour

Just a mild hint of radish in large, tender, deeply lobed leaves

Varieties

Currently there is a green- and a red-stemmed variety.

Sowing

Best from mid-September to end October; can also be sown January and February but it then crops for a shorter time before flowering in April.

Module-sowing

Three to five seeds, large and quick to germinate.

Spacing

Standard 22cm.

Leaf growth and picking

Growth is rapid; even the cotyledons are large and worth eating. Regular picking, by cutting or preferably pinching off individual leaves (being careful not to uproot the plant), should prolong growth until mid- to late April when flowering happens quite quickly. The white radish root is small and scarcely edible at this point, even though it may look tempting.

LETTUCE

Flavour

Pleasantly mild, especially by comparison with most other winter leaves. In my cool season mix I aim for about one quarter to one third lettuce.

Varieties

I pick *Grenoble Red* as a leaf lettuce and find it the most hardy and long-lived: it also has some slug- and mildew-resistance. *Freckles* and *Cocarde* are two other possibilities but they have a little less resistance to frost and mildew.

Sowing

September is good, early in its second week is often the best time.

Module-sowing

Two per module, thinned to the strongest plant after three or four weeks.

Spacing

Standard 22cm.

Leaf growth and picking

New leaves in autumn and winter are tender and usually small. Keep picking them because they will never grow big at that time of year, then from late February you will be amply rewarded with much larger, firmer and more easily picked leaves. Regular harvesting and correct watering will see robust growth until mid-June, by which time each plant may have produced over a hundred leaves.

MIBUNA

Flavour

Long, thin, elegant leaves are a little spicy but not too strong.

Varieties

Normally offered as mibuna.

Sowing

Mid- to late September.

Module-sowing
Average four seeds per module.

Spacing
Standard 22cm.

Leaf growth and picking
Lots of thin leaves make it tempting to cut across the top of plants, although patient picking of larger leaves will give more even harvests.

MITSUBA OR JAPANESE PARSLEY

Flavour
Exotic herby taste with plenty of parsley and celery flavours.

Varieties
Usually offered simply as 'mitsuba'.

Sowing
July to mid-August.

Module-sowing
Two or three seeds per module.

Spacing
Standard 22cm.

Leaf growth and picking
Mitsuba grows slowly from seed and in winter darkness, so only small pickings will be possible through the autumn and winter. Any flowering stalks should be removed and can be eaten. By March there should be many more leaves and only a few are needed to bring an unusual taste to the winter salad bowl. Plants can be kept going into summer by preventing flowering.

MIZUNA

Flavour
Long, tender leaves are mildly pungent.

Varieties
Not many to choose from; *Kyoto* is reliable.

Sowing
Late September for leaves before Christmas; early November for leaves afterwards.

Module-sowing
Average four seeds per module.

Spacing
Standard 22cm.

Leaf growth and picking
Mizuna grows extremely rapidly so needs picking quite soon after planting, unless you want large, long leaves. The latter are more prone to damage by severe frost. Although larger leaves can be regularly picked off, cutting is easier and then re-growth should be harvestable after another three or four weeks. Towards winter's end flowering stems will appear and they are delicious too. Mizuna's speed of growth counts against it in the stakes for longevity, three cuts is my maximum and the later ones are always thinner than the first

MUSTARD

Flavour
Decidedly peppery yet with a hint of sweetness, and a hot aftertaste.

Varieties
Four main ones are *Golden Streaks* for light green feathery leaves, *Ruby Streaks* for longer and even more indented leaves whose colour darkens to deep ruby in cold weather, *Red Giant* for oval-shaped leaves which rapidly grow large if allowed to, and *Green in the Snow* for more compact, hardy and hot leaves. Other varieties include *Osaka Purple*, similar to *Red Giant* but fleshier and less hardy, and *Southern Giant* which is a green version of its red cousin.

Sowing

Mid-September to end October, depending on when you want to start picking.

Module-sowing

About four seeds will produce nice clumps.

Spacing

Standard 22cm.

Leaf growth and picking

Large outer leaves can be individually picked and it is best to do this from November to February as re-growth is painfully slow at that time after cutting. Keep plants tidy by removing any yellowing leaves, then growth should become prolific by early spring when two or three cuts may be possible before flowering in early May. Cutting any flowering stalks will prolong the growth of smaller, thinner leaves.

PAK CHOI

Flavour

One of the mildest brassicas and with a pleasant crunch to its white stem.

Varieties

Joi Choi F1 is the hardiest one I know for overwintering.

Sowing

Mid-September gives time for plants to establish yet stay youthful enough to resist any hard frosts.

Module-sowing

Four or five seeds give a clump of plants whose leaves are not too large.

Spacing

Standard 22cm.

Leaf growth and picking

Keep picking regularly, unless you want larger leaves for stir-fry, although growth is slow in midwinter. Plants are fragile, shallow-rooted and need careful handling – sometimes I cut leaves individually, to disturb roots less. By mid-April there will be the first flower stems, which are nice to eat, and a diminishing number of leaves.

PEA SHOOTS

Flavour

A pea taste of summer, in winter.

Types

Tall growing peas make longer shoots but are a little less hardy than dwarf first early types. Tall peas should grow indoors from a late autumn sowing if winter is not exceptionally cold; otherwise sow in the New Year.

Sowing

As above – it depends on variety, location and weather. Early November is possible, or, for example, sow tall sugar snaps in a gently heated greenhouse in January for planting in February; there is room to experiment with other dates and varieties. Set mousetraps in greenhouses with germinating pea seeds.

Module-sowing

Three or four seeds per module.

Spacing

22-25cm allows sufficient room.

Leaf growth and picking

Pinch out about 7cm (3") of the main stem when plants are 25-30cm (10-12") high. For a while afterwards they will stop growing and then new shoots will appear from top and bottom of the existing and still-growing stem. Keep picking these increasingly plentiful shoots through late winter and spring, even with their flowers on – which also taste delicious. Shoots will crop into July if you keep picking them and a few peas are possible too from shoots that were missed.

ROCKET

Flavour

Spicy with a hot aftertaste, especially the larger leaves and those of older plants.

Varieties

Salad rocket has standard fleshy leaves; wild rocket has thinner, hotter ones. *Apollo* is a larger-leaved, less-lobed salad rocket.

Sowing

Mid-September to early October.

Module-sowing

Four or five seeds per module.

Spacing

Standard 22cm.

Leaf growth and picking

Early leaves are the largest; some growth continues steadily through all except the coldest winters and careful picking allows more rapid development of new leaves. Some leaves suffer fungal damage in midwinter and should be removed. By late March you should have plenty of rocket, and cutting is then possible as new growth in April is so rapid, at least until flowering from mid-April. Cutting flowering stems will encourage new leaf production until about mid-May.

SPINACH

Flavour

A welcome change to all the brassicas, it is somewhat metallic but also becomes sweeter during and just after cold weather, a real treat in February and March.

Varieties

Medania, with dark green leaves, is the most reliable for resisting frost, *Galaxy* has more upright and thinner leaves, while *Bordeaux* has pretty pale red stems and smaller, arrow-shaped leaves.

Sowing

September: early in the month is often better, giving more time for plants to grow. Earlier planting makes it more likely that spinach will outgrow any graying by slugs.

Module-sowing

Four to six seeds per module.

Spacing

Standard 22cm.

Leaf growth and picking

Keep picking all larger leaves and remove any that are holed by slugs and woodlice. The latter can cause much damage until plants grow away from them in late winter. Small winter leaves will become much larger and fleshier by March and you may have enough to let some grow into cooking spinach by April. Flowering of *Medania* is later than other salads, by mid-May on average.

TATSOI

Flavour

Similar to pak choi.

Varieties

There is choice here: the ground-hugging types such as *Rosette Pak Choi* are harder to pick, *Yukina Savoy* is larger-leaved and easier – check the small print in any description.

Sowing

Mid-September is best, to have plants established in the ground by mid-October.

Module-sowing

Four seeds on average.

Spacing

Standard 22cm.

Leaf growth and picking

Be wary of slugs as tatsoi is one of their favourites, especially when young, but it should grow away from occasional nibbles by mid-November. Leaves are best cut gently with a knife or pinched off carefully, as the root system of tatsoi is fragile and its leaf stems are firm. Growth is usually good in February and March, often ahead of other salads, but so is flowering – often by late March; growth finishes in early April.

WINTER PURSLANE (CLAYTONIA)

Flavour
Tender round leaves have a soft, delicate flavour and texture.

Varieties
I know only the generic winter purslane.

Sowing
September to October.

Module-sowing
A tiny pinch of the minuscule seeds usually gives a fine clump of leaves.

Spacing
Standard 22cm.

Leaf growth and picking
In a mild winter growth will be prolific. Cut stems when they are about 6-8cm (3") long and are holding large leaves above new growth at the centre of the clump, whence should come successive cuts at two- to four-week intervals. Cutting the larger leaves around plants' edges, rather than across the top, is less traumatic for them and ensures more rapid re-growth, with significant amounts of leaves from each clump, over the season as a whole. By March there may be some pretty and delicious white flowers as well, presaging the final seeding and smaller leaves of late April. Even more leaves can be obtained by cutting around the edges of clumps and leaving the central leaves to enlarge on a regular basis.

OTHER LEAVES

Next winter I look forward to trying a few different leaves, such as watercress, which I feel may be easier to harvest than land cress. I shall also be sowing some Chinese cabbage in mid- to late September, for growing as a leaf plant to keep picking, as I have a feeling it could be one of the most productive winter salads of all.

RESOURCES

ORGANISATIONS

Biodynamic Agriculture Association,
Painswick Inn Project,
Gloucester Street, Stroud GL5 1QG
www.biodynamic.org.uk
For biodynamic advice, books including calendars (see under
Publications, p.193), preparations and courses

Garden Organic (HDRA)
Ryton Gardens, Coventry CV8 3LG
www.gardenorganic.co.uk
For information, advice and events

www.OrganicCatalogue.com
The HDRA catalogue, for an extensive range of seeds and accessories

The Good Gardeners Association
4 Lisle Place, Wotton Under Edge,
Glos GL12 7AZ
www.goodgardeners.org.uk
For information on no-dig, nutrition and minerals in soil and food

The Royal Horticultural Society
80 Vincent Square,
London SW1P 2PE
Telephone 0845 250 5000
www.rhs.org.uk
For wide ranging, expert advice

SUPPLIERS

Charles Dowding
Lower Farm,
Shepton Montague,
Wincanton, Somerset BA9 8JG
www.charlesdowding.com
For monthly gardening advice and courses on vegetable growing.

The Herbary
161 Chapel Street,
Horningsham, Wiltshire BA12 7LU
www.beansandherbs.co.uk
For some unusual seeds, contact Pippa Rosen.

Implementations
PO Box 2568,
Nuneaton CV10 9YR
www.implementations.co.uk
For copper tools of high quality and information on Viktor Schauberger, who understood water better than anybody, see Publications, p.194.

Link-a-Bord
www.link-a-bord.com or telephone 01773 590556.
For window boxes and raised bed kits made from recycled pvc.

Oceangrown
info@oceangrown.co.uk or telephone 01749 812652.
For soil minerals from concentrated seawater.

Plants of Distinction
Abacus House,
Station Yard,
Needham Market IP6 8AS
www.plantsofdistinction.co.uk
For interesting seeds.

Rocket Gardens
www.rocketgardens.co.uk or telephone 01209 831468.
For vegetable plants and 'instant' salad gardens.

Seeds of Italy
C3 Phoenix Industrial Estate,
Rosslyn Crescent, Harrow HA1 2SP
www.seedsofitaly.com
Sell Franchi seeds – especially good for chicory and endive.

SEER Centre
Ceanghline,
Straloch Farm,
Enochdu,
Perthshire PH10 7PJ
www.seercentre.org.uk
For information on minerals and rock dust, and sales of rock dust.

Tamar Organics
Tavistock Woodlands Estate,
Gulworthy,
Tavistock PL19 8JE
www.tamarorganics.co.uk
For a wide range of organic seeds and sundries.

West Riding Organics
www.wrorganics.co.uk or telephone 01484 609171
For organic potting compost which includes rock dust.

PUBLICATIONS

The Biodynamic Sowing and Planting Calendar
by Maria Thun
Published annually in Britain by Floris Books (see BDAA, p.191);
sells 100,000 copies worldwide each year.

Gardening and Planting by the Moon
by Nick Kollerstrom
Published annually by Quantum

Lunar planting calendar
Tidegraph Ltd,
50 The Street,
Firle, East Sussex BN8 6LQ
www.lunarorganics.com

The Moon and the Growth of Plants
by L. Kolisko
First published in 1936 and later reprinted by
Kolisko Archive Publications, 1978

Organic Gardening: the Natural No-dig Way
by Charles Dowding
Green Books, 2007

The Organic Salad Garden
by Joy Larkcom
Frances Lincoln, 2001

Viktor Schauberger: A Life of Learning From Nature
by Jane Cobbald
Floris Books, 2006

Index

Also by Charles Dowding:

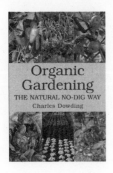

ORGANIC GARDENING
The natural no-dig way

"One of our most respected vegetable growers . . . Now ordinary gardeners can benefit from his years of practical experience, growing great vegetables in harmony with Mother Earth." – Joy Larkcom

"Charles is a passionate and accomplished gardener who grows vegetables of amazing flavour." – Raymond Blanc

In **Organic Gardening**, Charles Dowding shares the philosophy, tips and techniques which have enabled him to run a successful organic garden supplying local restaurants and shops for over 25 years:

- Forget the rules: 'received wisdom' about gardening is surprisingly inaccurate. Understand better what is going on in the soil and with your plants, in your own garden and climate, and work out your own methods instead.

- Respect and encourage life as much as you can, chiefly by spreading good compost or manure.

- There is no need to dig in compost and manure – just spread it on top and let worms take it in. Digging can harm soil structure, and is not helpful to plants.

- You can reduce weeding to a little hand-weeding or hoeing every ten days.

Based on his experience of a system of permanent slightly-raised beds, Charles takes you through a delicious variety of fruit and vegetables: what to choose, when to plant and harvest, and how best to avoid pests and diseases. The book includes recipes to inspire you to culinary heights with your fresh-picked produce.

ISBN 978 1 903998 91 5   £10.95 paperback

For our complete catalogue, see www.greenbooks.co.uk